A Miracle in Progress is a very touching, heart-warming collection of stories about the love among the volunteers and customers of the Duneland Resale shop. I have read the book, and it excellently captures the feelings and emotions of all involved. Thank you for sharing your experiences. I, too, have been blessed.
~ **Deane Janjecic, retired English teacher**

Decades from now people can read this book and learn how this phenomenal institution was founded in our town. What a wonderful place!
~ **Joan Costello, Westchester Township History Museum Registrar, and Duneland Historical Society President**

Ann Howard's stories of life in the Duneland Resale shop opens secret doors to miracles in our midst. The ordinary becomes extraordinary. The lost are found. And even the reader is brushed by angels' wings. These stories made me laugh, they made me cry, and they made me believe.
~ **Margaret Amundson, retired German/English teacher**

These amazing Resale shop angels are a great reminder that giving back is part of life's purpose. My spirit is inspired by these stories.
~ **Beth (Howard) Roach, business consultant**

A Miracle in Progress
Duneland Resale: Faith in Action

A celebration of the miraculous journey of Duneland Resale and accounts of miracles witnessed at Resale and beyond

Ann Howard

Resale blessings! Ann

All proceeds from the sale of this book benefit Duneland Resale.

A Miracle in Progress

*A celebration of the miraculous
journey of Duneland Resale
and accounts of miracles
witnessed at Resale and beyond*

Duneland United Churches Resale, Inc.
801 Broadway
Chesterton, IN 46304
219-926-1404

www.dunelandresale.com
Facebook: Duneland Resale

Copyright © 2010 by Ann Howard
and Duneland Resale
All Rights Reserved

No part of this book may be reproduced in any
form without permission.

Printed in the U.S.A.
InstantPublisher.com, 2010

ISBN: 978-0-578-07340-8

Front cover, upper left photo: left to right: volunteers Jack Schoenfelder, Dan Johnston, Ann Howard, and Bob Ruppenkamp; top right: Frank Sessa; lower left photo: Kay Johnson (left), Judy Ross; lower right: Joy Johnston.
Back cover: third Duneland Resale shop, 534 Broadway, Chesterton, Indiana.

Duneland United Churches Resale, Inc. Mission Statement

Duneland Resale is a God-centered, not-for-profit organization of volunteers dedicated to helping others. Quality used merchandise which is donated to us is recycled and sold. Proceeds are used to assist service agencies, missions, and community needs.

> Do all the good you can,
> By all the means you can,
> In all the ways you can,
> In all the places you can,
> At all the times you can,
> To all the people you can,
> As long as ever you can.
> ~ John Wesley

For I was hungry and you gave me food, I was thirsty and you gave me drink, I was a stranger and you welcomed me, I was naked and you clothed me, I was sick and you visited me, I was in prison and you came to me.
~ Jesus' words in Matthew 25: 35-36 (RSV)

Dedication

This book is dedicated with love to the nearly one hundred loyal volunteers who have faithfully donated their time and energy to the Resale mission. Their contributions and special gifts have made this mission what it is today.

We also dedicate this book to the Mission Committee of St. John's United Church, the people who initiated the idea of a resale shop. With hard work, determination, courage, and strong faith, they developed the project and opened the first Resale shop.

In addition, with appreciation this book is dedicated to Dan and Joy Johnston, our Executive Director and Volunteer Coordinator, both members of the St. John's Mission Committee who founded Duneland Resale. Their dedication and patient direction has contributed immeasurably to the shop's success and growth, and their example and caring about each of us has transformed our group of volunteers into a loving family.

Most of all we dedicate this book to God, the one who inspires and sustains us and gives us miracles along our journey.

Opposite page, top left to right to bottom: first shop (104 N. Calumet), second shop (221 N. Calumet), third shop (534 Broadway), and fourth/current Duneland Resale shop (801 Broadway).

Acknowledgements

~ by Ann Howard, volunteer

To the entire Resale family and to our customers and friends – thank you for your input and for sharing your wonderful stories. Special thanks to those who wrote their own stories. Without your contributions, there could be no book. Therefore, this is not *my* book, but instead it is *our* book. I am *but* the messenger.

To Margaret Amundson, my writing partner and friend – I can never thank you enough for editing this book. You separated the wheat from the chaff. You pared down my verbosity and you weeded out my extraneous and excessive commas. You laughed and shed tears in all the right places. Most of all, you cheered me on when I needed encouragement. Margaret, you're the best!

To Millie Samuelson – you are a true Earth Angel! You took time out from your own writing to edit this book, mentor me through my struggle to format the book, and give me so many tips and your expert advice along the way. Your support is one of the miracles I have witnessed. I could never have done the job without you. Thank you from me and from all of us at Duneland Resale.

To Dan Johnston, my sincere thanks for ALL the marvelous photos in this book. Thanks also to Tom Clements for the photos of the first Resale shop.

Special thanks to all those friends who proofread and edited the book: Deane Janjecic, English teacher extraordinaire, Tom Clements, who served on the St. John's Mission Committee when Resale was born; Dr. Daniel Keilman, fellow volunteer, for keeping me on task; Wendy Marciniak, St. John's Elder and cheerleader for Resale from the beginning, for proofreading and also helping with book promotion and publicity; Joan Costello, for her expertise and advice; and finally, my daughter Beth Roach, who enthusiastically read the book and offered insightful suggestions.

The *Chesterton Tribune* deserves special thanks for their continuing support by including many pictures and stories of our activities in the newspaper. The entire Duneland community has supported us by their donations, patronage, and encouraging words and prayers. We thank you all.

To my husband Frank who so patiently supported my work on this book in so many ways: for never once complaining about having late meals or no meals, for ignoring the cobwebs which appeared here and there during my periods of preoccupation with the book, for researching the intricacies of the computer programs which often baffled me, for rushing to my aid when I called out for help, and for never once doubting that the project would be successfully completed – my love and thanks!

A Miracle in Progress

Contents

Dedication
Acknowledgements
Introduction
Why This Book Was Written by Ann Howard
History by Ann Howard
Beehive by Ann Howard
Welcome to Duneland Resale! by Ann Howard

ONE: WHY WE ARE HERE.....................28
Why Are We Here? told by volunteers
An Epiphany by Ann Howard
A Place Where I Belong told by Peggy Dalton
Why I Am Here by Daniel Keilman
Where People Care by Phyllis Bishop
A Perfect Fit by Christi Kalbe
Worker Bees by Phyllis Bishop

TWO: EARTH ANGELS........................62
Tornado by Ann Howard
A Band of Angels told by Alice Perney
A Random Act by Pat Amstutz
We Are His Hands by Margo Ulrich
Just A Small Thing told by a volunteer
People Who Care told by a volunteer
Earth Angels All Around Us by Ann Howard

THREE: MIRACLES OF HEALING...............82
God-Connections by Ann Howard
The Roller Coaster by Paula Stolk
Turning Point by Dan Keilman
An Unexpected Angel by Jerry Ward and Pastor Cathy Allison
Fred Wright by Pat Wright

A Miracle in Progress

Mary Ann Wright by Pat Wright
The Miracle of Gary told by Joy & Dan Johnston

FOUR: GLIMPSES OF GOD.....................108
Miraculous Moments told by volunteers
A Delightful Surprise told by a volunteer
A Timely Blessing told by a volunteer
An Angel on My Shoulder by Brandon Fero
Life Is a Miracle! Breathing! Seeing! Hearing!
Reproducing! Loving! by Dan Keilman
A Bounty of Blessings told by a volunteer
How All the Pieces Fit Together by Ann Howard
Life Saver told by Jack Schoenfelder
In the Right Place by Kim Goldak
Slated for Success by Ann Howard
Miracles and More Miracles told by Mary Louise Reey
A Treasure Found by Wendy Marciniak
A Christmas Blessing told by Aleta Ailes
Ask and Ye Shall Receive told by Dan Johnston
The Miracle of Love by Daniel Keilman
The Message by Ann Howard
Special Delivery by Ann Howard

FIVE: A GOOD LAUGH........................155
If the Shoe Fits and Whatever Goes Around told by Dan Johnston
One Man's Trash by Ann Howard
Tug o' War by Ann Howard
Lifeline Tales told by Nancy Ruffing
Trapped! by Ann Howard
Wind Power told by Dan Johnston
The Episode of the Traveling Pants by Ann Howard
The Tale of the Irresistible Blouse by Ann Howard
Back Door Brigade by Ann Howard
Sanford by Ann Howard

A Miracle in Progress

Snippets told by volunteers, Dan Johnston, Ed Lewandowski, Chuck Swickard, & Bonnie Flatz

SIX: DONATIONS. 184
Something Good told by a Resale donor
Donations de Jour by Ann Howard
Tee Shirts de Jour by Ann Howard

SEVEN: SPECIAL PEOPLE, SPECIAL FRIENDS. . . 195
Many Hats and Herding Cats by Ann Howard
Regarding Sanford . . . by Ann Howard
Pastor Ed told by Joy Johnston & volunteers
True Success by Ann Howard
The Hungry Are Fed by Ann Howard
Alyce by Ann Howard
Miss Martha by Ann Howard
Charlie's Gift by Ann Howard
Walking Softly told by Joy Johnston

EIGHT: REFLECTIONS. 216
Teamwork by Ann Howard
Celebration by Ann Howard
All Work and No Play? Not for Us! by Ann Howard
Behind the Scenes by Joy Johnston

NINE: JUST THE FACTS. 229
Did You Know... Volunteer handbook, Joy Johnston
Recycling Goods to Do Good Volunteer handbook
Where Does the Money Go? Volunteer handbook
Donations – Duneland Resale Outreach Mission, Volunteer Handbook
Volunteer Service

A Miracle in Progress

Introduction

This book celebrates the incredible journey of Duneland Resale. We volunteers want to share the excitement and passion that all those who have been a part of this mission have felt. You will learn about the Resale mission operation and goals, and you will meet some of our volunteers, customers and special friends.

Being involved with the "Resale" mission has strengthened the faith in God of many of our volunteers who have witnessed numerous miracles, both large and small. We hope that you, the reader, will be inspired by their accounts and also those of our customers and friends who have shared their own miracles, experienced at Duneland Resale and in other places as well.

It is said that one always gets back more than one gives, and these words have never rung more true than at Duneland Resale. Volunteering there continues to be a rich and rewarding experience for all of us. It is our hope that as you read the stories, you, too, will feel the joy, empathy and awe we have felt and that your hearts will be as touched by our accounts of these experiences as ours have been by living them.

A Miracle in Progress

Why This Book Was Written

~ by Ann Howard

During the years that I have volunteered at Duneland Resale, I cannot count the number of times that I have been awed by both large and small miracles I have witnessed there. After one such experience, I said aloud, "This place is truly amazing! Someone should write a book about it and what goes on here."

Another volunteer said, "That's a good idea. Why don't you do it?"

Admittedly, I was taken aback by her comment, but quickly recovered. *Why not?* I thought, then said, "Well, I guess I could do it. Okay. . . I will."

Thus the idea of a book about Resale and all the miracles happening there was born. The book would include the shop's history, operation, people, and other pertinent facts. The idea was simple enough and I began.

First I asked volunteers why they had decided to volunteer at Resale, and then I asked them to share their stories about Resale – about the miracles they had witnessed. Progress was slow, with only a few stories coming in, and I worried that I would not have enough material to fill a book.

A Miracle in Progress

As their responses trickled in, a few inspired volunteers told me about miracles they had seen in their own lives as well as those at Resale. Several customers heard about the book and came to me with their stories. The seed was planted. Again I thought *Why not? Why not include some of these other, yet related miracles?*

Then customers and volunteers related their humorous stories about Resale. Others gave me miraculous stories of angels among us, and I became aware of the stories that were developing around me. The idea of the book began to inspire the volunteers, and soon I realized that I had gathered many wonderful stories which must be included in the book. The book seemed to be growing all on its own, and so I nurtured it, letting it grow into the book you are about to read.

A Miracle in Progress

History

~ *by Ann Howard, volunteer*

This book is about Duneland Resale, the "little shop" that, with God at the helm, COULD. This amazing story began in 2000 with the inspired and forward-thinking Mission Committee of St. John's United Church in Chesterton, Indiana: Linda Gray, Chairperson; Florian Steciuch; Dan and Joy Johnston, Duneland Resale's Director and Volunteer Coordinator; Joni Wainovich; William Sievert; Bonnie and Jack Hopper; and Tom Clements.

The committee was extremely concerned about the increasing number of people in the Duneland area whose basic needs were not being met. Their question: What was the best way to provide that help?

Inspired by her sister's work in a church-sponsored resale shop, Linda Gray proposed the idea of a similar shop in Chesterton. After much discussion and prayer, this team decided to open a resale shop to help those in need in the Duneland community and beyond.

The Presbyterian Women of Valparaiso eagerly encouraged the cloning of their successful mission and provided much of the groundwork for the upcoming birth of Duneland Resale.

A Miracle in Progress

St. John's Mission Committee proposed the idea to their congregation, who, after serious consideration, voted their support and then allocated $2,000 from their mission budget toward the start-up funds for the Resale mission.

In addition, the Independent Order of Odd Fellows donated $1,000 to the mission. Armed with $3,000 and their faith, the group moved forward. Later they were given a grant by the national United Church of Christ and a donation from the Chesterton First United Methodist Church. Although the majority of the original shop volunteers were from St. John's church, they were soon joined by many others.

A Resale mission statement was created, details ironed out, and a name chosen. On March 24, 2001, the doors of United Churches Resale were opened at 104 North Calumet Avenue in Chesterton with Linda Gray serving as Director.

It was soon obvious that the task would need many hands for completion. Neighboring church members gladly pitched in to keep the dream alive. Ed Mitchell, pastor of the Porter United Methodist Church, was one of those volunteers. He contributed countless hours and immeasurable services to this mission.

In a short time, the mission evolved into an ecumenical endeavor, uniting many Duneland churches via their Resale volunteers. On April 4, 2002, the shop was detached from St. John's

A Miracle in Progress

church and was incorporated as Duneland United Churches Resale, Inc, a not-for-profit organization.

And the rest is not simply history, but instead, an unfolding story, rich with blessings and miracles. The stories of some of these awe-inspiring events as well as many other facts about Duneland Resale are included in this book.

**The first Resale Shop on North Calumet.
Left to right: Joy Johnston, Tim Pell, Linda Gray,
Bonnie Hopper, Nancy Kahaian, Joni Wainovich.**

Duneland Resale soon outgrew its original space on 104 North Calumet and moved across the street to a larger store at 221 North Calumet. In

A Miracle in Progress

July of 2004 the shop relocated again, moving several blocks away to a much larger building which it now owns, mortgage free, at 534 Broadway. It remained in that location for five years. In its short history, this "little shop" had outgrown three retail spaces. In 2009 it moved to its present home at 801 Broadway, formerly Wiseway Foods.

Dan and Joy Johnston celebrate the opening of the fourth Duneland Resale shop on Broadway.

Although Duneland Resale owns the entire building, which has a total area of 25,000 square feet, its retail shopping area occupies the east half. Westchester Neighbors Food Pantry has already joined Resale as its first guest on the west side of the building, and Joan Knibbs' Duneland Medical Equipment Closet recently became its second guest. The next phase of the vision includes

A Miracle in Progress

housing a wellness clinic and a community meeting room. The community services will form an umbrella agency called Duneland Community Alliance.

In our first ten years, the Resale mission, which now has volunteers who represent over twenty Duneland area churches, has donated over $1,180,000 in cash and merchandise to various individuals, agencies and causes, many of which are listed in the "Where Does the Money Go?" and "Duneland Resale Outreach Mission" chapters.

Ministers representing the more than twenty Duneland area churches involved with Resale cut the ribbon to celebrate the dedication of the shop at 801 Broadway.

Although most contributions have been directed to this community and the Duneland area, support has also been given to other missions farther afield, which include Heifer International,

A Miracle in Progress

aid to Katrina and Haiti hurricane victims, as well as several other national and international missions.

The continuing success of Duneland Resale results from a remarkable three-fold effort. First, community members donate quality items to be sold at fair prices; second, our volunteers, who now number almost 100, manage and run the shop; and finally, loyal customers continue to buy our merchandise.

We know that God has greatly blessed our efforts. With His help, our volunteers continue "to render loving service toward humankind." We have no doubt that Duneland Resale is a miracle in progress.

Volunteers take a break at the fourth Resale shop, 801 Broadway, Chesterton, Indiana.
Photo courtesy of the Chesterton Tribune.

A Miracle in Progress

Beehive

~ by Ann Howard, volunteer

Duneland Resale is much like a beehive. Early in the morning outside the hive, you see only a few bees as they flit about, carrying out wares for display and preparing for the busy day. Soon they go inside and all is quiet as they join their hearts and minds in prayer. Then the front doors are opened and the business of the hive begins.

More and more bees gather, swooping toward the hive, then inside, until swarms of them dart enthusiastically from item to item while others fly in and out of the shop. The air is electric with excitement. Shopper bees hover as they browse among the shelves and examine the merchandise, while others zip around to greet friends. Many, delighted with the treasures they have found, soar triumphantly out the doors.

Worker bees buzz buzz about, welcoming and helping the shoppers, restocking shelves, checking out and bagging purchases and carrying out the shoppers' bargains. The hive is abuzz with activity.

But there is something else happening here. In the background, barely audible above the din in the sales area, there is a buzzing which becomes louder and louder as you approach the double doors at the back. The doors open and you are

A Miracle in Progress

engulfed in a whirl of movement and sound. The buzzing has escalated to a near-roar and there is action everywhere. This area is called, simply, the back room, but it is much, much more than that. You have reached the inner chamber – the pulse, the heart of the hive – and you are overwhelmed with the energy around you.

At first glance, the scene looks chaotic but, as you watch, you notice that there is an organization and pattern to the activity. Every worker bee has a purpose, a specific job, which contributes to the overall workings of the hive. Each labors in his or her own place – examining, sorting, pricing and tagging donations – while others flit back and forth, loading and unloading baskets of wares for the sales area. As the pace increases, the buzz becomes deafening.

Outside this chamber, at the back entrance, other bees welcome and assist those bringing in their donations. In addition, they are constantly called to carry out the heavier purchases for customers. These faithful and tireless bees, vital to the working of the hive, bear the heaviest loads, going in and out, in and out, all day long.

Of course, in this, as in any hive, there is a Queen bee, and ours is Joy Johnston. But make no mistake – she is no ordinary queen, who sits on her throne and directs the workers to do her bidding. Instead, this Queen bee is one of the busiest workers, constantly sorting items and helping the

A Miracle in Progress

others with their tasks, while coordinating all activity and cheering her fellow workers on. Her sense of humor and vitality keep the spirits of the rest uplifted during their busy day. Following her in flight is impossible, for she is everywhere.

Unlike other hives, this one also has a King, or Manager bee, Dan Johnston, who oversees all activity inside as well as outside the hive. Constantly in motion, buzzing about here and there, he represents the hive within his community and in neighboring communities. Certainly, he is as busy as the Queen bee – perhaps busier – going about his countless jobs quietly, but efficiently, helping, guiding and encouraging others while seeing that all runs smoothly. Busy as he is, he remains a kind, calm, and steady leader who sets the tone for the entire hive.

As the workday progresses and the whirl of activity and noise builds to a dizzying pace, a steady rhythm and order prevail. Not surprisingly, occasional tension disrupts the hive, but invariably laughter lightens the mood. A strong sense of family and dedication to a common purpose bond the workers into an effective team.

As the day winds down, the din subsides, the bees' energy wanes and the pace visibly slows. At last, after the swarm of bees dissipates, a few, the King and Queen and several others, stay behind to close the hive before heading home for a well-deserved rest. They are exhausted, but satisfied

A Miracle in Progress

and truly grateful for the many accomplishments of the day.

Donations from a generous community have been processed by these volunteers, then sold, with the profits going where they are needed. These bees have witnessed answered prayers. As a result of their labor, some who are hungry are fed, some who need shelter are housed and some who are lonely find friends. Certainly lives have been improved. And the worker bees, themselves, have been uplifted by being a part of this miracle in progress. Thanks be to God.

Worker bee Don Pratt (right) and his helper Keith Simms (left) haul metal to be recycled.

A Miracle in Progress

Welcome to Duneland Resale!

~ by Ann Howard, volunteer

It seems appropriate to introduce the first people many customers see as they enter Resale, our two greeters, Bill Gland and Aleta Ailes.

"Well, hello! And how are you today? Welcome to Duneland Resale!" Bill has twinkling eyes and a grin so wide that customers know he is sincerely delighted to welcome them. It is easy to imagine this charming gentleman in a top hat and tails, bowing to those who enter.

He eagerly answers the shoppers' questions and often chats with them as they browse about. As they are leaving, he sees them off with a warm farewell, "Thank you so much for shopping here. Now, you have a wonderful day!" Undoubtedly Bill makes our customers know that they are appreciated.

Bill Gland officially greets Resale customers.

A Miracle in Progress

Aleta Ailes is affectionately nicknamed our Butterfly Girl. Not only does she wear butterfly barrettes, clothing and jewelry, but she reminds us of a colorful butterfly in flight, bringing sunshine wherever she lands.

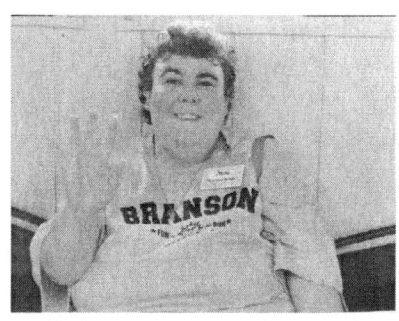

Aleta Ailes gives a welcoming wave.

When Aleta arrives with her contagious grin, her kind words and warm hugs, smiles spontaneously appear all around her. It is impossible to be unhappy in her presence. Whether she is greeting customers or doing routine tasks around the shop, she radiates joy and hope. Her faith in God is an inspiration to each of us. To quote Joy Johnston: "Aleta is an example of God's perfect love."

Now that you have met Resale's official greeters, please do consider yourself officially welcomed!

A Miracle in Progress

ONE
Why We Are Here

Why Are We Here?

~ as told by volunteers to Ann Howard, volunteer

Volunteers were asked, "Why did you decide to volunteer at Duneland Resale?" and "Why do you continue to volunteer here?" These volunteers gave their thoughtful and varied responses. Please meet some of them and read their comments.

Some of our happy Duneland Resale volunteers.

A Miracle in Progress

When Evelyn Brickner came to the shop with a donation, her friend Eleanor Lindquist, who was a volunteer, said, "Why don't you and your friend Deloris volunteer here, too?" That's all it took.

Evelyn called Deloris Weitzel, and the rest is history. Working at Duneland Resale is habit-forming, and we are grateful that this energetic duo has stayed on to keep the Housewares Department humming. They have earned the nicknames "Sparkle and Shine" because everything that leaves their hands is bright and shining.

"Sparkle and Shine" Deloris Weitzel (left) and Evelyn Brickner (right)

One day I was standing in the kitchen with Dean Recktenwall, who is one of our busiest volunteers. He and I were admiring the table full

A Miracle in Progress

of delectable foods – Italian beef sandwiches, salads and cookies. "Say," I said, "I've been meaning to ask you why you volunteer here."

He laughed, pointed at the table and said, "Will work for food!

"Dean, in addition to working at the back door and doing various other jobs at Resale, has spent countless hours painting the interiors and exteriors of both of our shops at 534 and 801 Broadway. His generous donation of time and work is noteworthy because we have it on good authority that Dean truly HATES to paint!

Joyce, Dean's wife, spends hours and hours diligently sorting through countless knick-knacks. After scrubbing a less than pristine donation, she chuckled and said, "Why do I continue to work here? Why?" Sometimes I ask myself that very question!" "No, really," she added, "I have many, many positive reasons for staying."

Frank Sessa, former owner of The Cobbler's Bench and Bootery and later Frank's Shoe Repair, is now Resale's resident cobbler and shoe expert – our "sole" man. The shoe department has never looked better! Frank helps in other areas as well, and customers and volunteers appreciate his gracious, friendly manner. Frank said, "There is a group of dedicated hard-working citizens at Duneland Resale. They make this community a great place to live, and there's absolutely no place I'd rather be."

A Miracle in Progress

Marlene Westergren wrote: "The first time I met Danny Johnston, we were in the seventh grade . . . so, add it up – friends for over 50 years. I left town for 30 years and had no clue as to Dan's whereabouts. . . . Upon returning to Chesterton and after a visit to Duneland Resale, I saw Dan and he said, 'Come volunteer'. . . of course, Joy and Dan have earned the respect of our community by being so tireless in their great dedication to Duneland Resale. I'm proud to be a part of it!"

Judy Ross, our energetic celebration/party planner and capable all-round helper, said, "Duneland Resale means a lot to me. It has been one of my greatest passions ever since I began volunteering at our first shop. I know that it is a great way to help touch the lives of others. Also, very important to me are the wonderful volunteers and customers, who have become my friends."

Dr. Dan Keilman, a volunteer and counselor at Resale, wrote the following: "For over 70 years I have been looking forward to being in Heaven. I have found Heaven and many true saints at Resale."

Martha Miller, a fine writer of nature and children's books and one of our early volunteers who loved the Resale mission, moved to Florida, but she never forgot about Duneland Resale. Even after moving, she continued her support by sending huge boxes of donations back to us.

A Miracle in Progress

"A few years ago I stopped to check out the shop," said Alice Zink, a petite dynamo who bags customers' purchases and works on the sales floor. "Everyone was so busy, and they seemed happy to be there. I thought this was the place for me when I retired. I've met and made good friends, and I'm so happy I stopped at Duneland Resale that day."

Don Pratt, who works at the back door as well as helping in numerous other areas, claims that he is hanging around, just hoping for a transfer. When asked why he wants a transfer, he maintains that everybody in the back room is crazy.

Possibly he is referring to shenanigans such as those with monkeys, rubber ping pong balls and other unexpected objects flying through the air. However, there is unconfirmed speculation that he is still unhappy with us for accidentally selling his boots and coat while he slaved away at the back door. His dry sense of humor keeps everyone in a good mood.

Tim Oberle, our busy tagger, back room helper and expert knitter, says that he volunteers because it helps keep him off the streets. . . on Thursdays and/or Saturdays.

Theresa Diffenbach, another versatile back room volunteer, said, "Recently I was looking for a pair of blue shoes to wear to my grandson's Bar Mitzvah and found them at Resale for only $2.00.

A Miracle in Progress

Perfect! I'm new at the resale shop and love it and the people."

Sheila Gardner, a busy volunteer who cashiers and cheerfully works wherever needed, said, "I had known about Duneland Resale through Ann Howard for years before we moved to Chesterton, and once we moved it was one of the first places we went. I have wanted to volunteer there ever since, but due to my work schedule, I was unable to do so until a few months ago.

My first day there was such a spiritual experience, starting with the opening prayer, the welcoming from everyone, and the great people who shop there. I get a lot more out of it than I give, and it truly is a spiritual experience where the work of God is done continually."

"Three years ago, I met Dan Johnston when he picked up a hospital bed from my home. He was very pleasant and explained to me about the mission of Duneland Resale. I was so impressed that I decided I wanted to be a part of this wonderful organization. I have enjoyed meeting so many great people and I feel good knowing that I am helping others," says Delores Rubinate, our amiable cashier and sales floor volunteer.

Bill Ong stays on because he "just can't find a way out!" We know he is kidding. Our capable treasurer and back door volunteer must love his job because he does it every week and he does it so

A Miracle in Progress

well. Furthermore, Zella Olsen's story confirms our view of his devotion to Resale.

Zella claims that Nona and Bill Ong practically broke her arm by twisting it so hard, urging her to volunteer. She enjoys the people at Duneland Resale and volunteering at the shop in several different areas makes her feel young. She supports Resale not only by her many hours of working, but also by her frequent shopping there.

Zella's husband Roy volunteers because Nona, Bill and Zella would not give up on him (another arm twisted!). They asked him to join the ever-busy electrical team, Chuck Swickard and Mark Ligda. Roy has a good sense of humor and he is able to stand up to the lively banter in the back room.

In the early days of Resale, Joan Sitar's brother Roger Leady told her that Resale was a fun place to work. Once she filled in for a cashier and discovered he was right. It really was fun! Later she came on board full time.

She and Zella are a busy, versatile twosome, often working together on baby items, crafts, toys, cashiering or in any other capacity where they are needed. At different times Joan and also Joan Jasen were chairmen of the shoe department. Each was most appropriately nicknamed "Joan of Arch."

Mary Keane, another of our friendly and helpful cashiers, enjoys the camaraderie at the

A Miracle in Progress

shop and she feels good about all that Duneland Resale does. Besides, she claims to have the best selection of Legos in town!

Our cheerful greeter Aleta Ailes volunteers at Resale because she loves helping other people and giving hope. She wrote the following:

>**H**elping
>**O**ther
>**P**eople
>**E**very day
>
>**G**reat
>**O**utstanding
>**D**eeds

Ruth Schilla, who did alterations at the local cleaners for twenty years, finally retired. Free at last, she was ready for adventure, for new challenges, but she was at a loss as to what those challenges would be. In fact, she was in limbo. *What to do?*

She talked to friends, but no one had an idea that inspired her. Her accountant suggested that volunteering would be a meaningful activity for her as well as a service to the community.

Volunteering? Yes, of course, she had read the newspaper articles about worthwhile volunteer efforts, and there were certainly places in town

A Miracle in Progress

needing volunteer help. In fact, there were too many places, and she was still in a quandary. *Where did she belong?*

Frequent newspaper articles about Duneland Resale sparked her interest, and she liked what she read. She decided Duneland Resale was the place for her to volunteer.

Lu Paulson, one of our seasoned volunteers who welcomes everyone to the front desk with a winning smile, said, "I've loved this place from the minute I began working here. Everyone is so congenial. I've met so many people whom I'd never had the pleasure of knowing otherwise." (Anyone who knows Lu knows the pleasure is all ours.)

Lee Amstutz, who volunteers at the back door, says, "I work at Resale because it's good exercise!" Good exercise is an understatement for what he does. He keeps himself and the shop in good shape because he is one of the tireless volunteers who do the back-breaking work of hauling the heaviest items into and out of the shop.

He and the others at the back door have by far the most strenuous jobs at Resale. Furthermore, he works at the back door for three days each week!

A Miracle in Progress

Pat and Lee Amstutz, dedicated volunteers

Lee's wife Pat is a skilled cashier and also our extremely busy and capable books chairman. She stepped up to replace Carole Phegley, our hard-working books/collectibles chairman, who has now retired. Pat described her reasons for volunteering at Resale in this way:

Renewing acquaintances of friends and students
Expanding my circle of Christian friends
Seeing smiles of those who find what they want
Assisting others
Learning some new skills
Explaining our purpose

Spending time in service to the community
Hearing positive comments and appreciation
Opportunities to reach out to those in need
Praying together, starting each day on a high note

A Miracle in Progress

Lou Roberts and Becky Dunbar are two of our hard-working volunteers who do their very necessary work behind the scenes. They take home our soiled clothing items and launder and iron them to make them attractive and saleable.

Lou thought the concept of a resale shop for charity was a good idea, but she had no time to work at the shop on a regular basis. She said, "The people volunteering at Duneland Resale were so enthusiastic, and their attitude was contagious. I wanted to do something, too, for the cause."

Becky also thought that Resale's mission was most worthwhile, but she had no time to volunteer on a weekly shift. "I chose to do Resale laundry and ironing at home at my convenience, and I've done it ever since the beginning."

Bill Gland, our congenial greeter, said, "Believe me, it's no secret to my family and friends that joining this dedicated caring group of men and women at the local resale shop. . . was one of the most satisfying and heart-warming decisions this old man has ever made! They're all very special people!"

Evelyn Komenas, an industrious back room volunteer, feels that those who profess their faith miss the point if they do not act on their beliefs. She volunteers at Resale because it is a place where people put their faith into action.

Lil and Chuck Swickard, along with their daughter Tammie Fero, joined the Resale team

A Miracle in Progress

mainly because the mission began in their church. They decided to "get involved" and made it a family affair. All three of them have been faithful, dedicated workers since the early days of Resale.

Lil is the busy "Linens Lady" and Chuck works wonders in the electronics department. Tammie, truly a "Jack of all trades" at the shop, is currently co-chairing Baby Clothing with Nancy Ruffing, and she often helps at the cash register. This family has continued at Resale because they feel good about what Resale does in helping the entire community.

Lil and Chuck Swickard (left), their grandson Brandon Fero and their daughter Tammie Fero make being volunteers at Resale into a family affair.

Anne and Pat Inherst found themselves with some extra time on their hands and wanted to do

A Miracle in Progress

something worthwhile. Anne began volunteering at Resale, and Pat joined soon after. They worked full-time and tirelessly for nearly two years, until Pat developed a health problem and family needs consumed their time.

Anne said they felt at home at Duneland Resale because the people there were so friendly and made them feel as if they were part of a large family. When Anne comes to Resale now, she finds that, instead of shopping, she spends her time visiting and enjoying a reunion with friends.

According to recent statistics, the average volunteer stays in the same place for three years. We are delighted that most of our volunteers have remained with us for much longer, and some have been at the shop since the beginning. Recently Joy Johnston joked that our volunteers are just like the line in the song "Hotel California": "You can check in any time you want, but you can never leave..."

The following is a list of many reasons our volunteers give for being at Duneland Resale and continuing to volunteer there:

Benefits given to those who are ill
My offspring learn about missions.
Fun work
Life purpose
Caring new friends
Good stewards of proceeds

A Miracle in Progress

Lifeline benefits
Ecumenical blending of community
Second Chance choir
Gala, great fun!
Seeing Santa at Christmas sale
Flu shots
Group outings
Earth conscious customers
Resale helped when I was in need.
The pay is out of this world!
Fellowship
Helping others
Laughter
Resale recycles Duneland's goods.
Free Christian counseling
Actions speak louder than words.
Rebuilding Together team
Relay for Life Team
Hurricane Helpers
Many hands make light work.
Cancer research funding
Putting our faith into action
I'm retired. . . flexible hours.
Fringe benefits!
I want to give back to Duneland.
Angel tree

A Miracle in Progress

"Where else but Resale can you take your dog to work?" thinks Jason Kremke.

Left to right: Volunteers Peggy Dalton, Deanna Kronland, Nancy Ruffing, and Mark Ligda enjoy clowning around at Duneland Resale.

A Miracle in Progress

An Epiphany

~ *by Ann Howard, volunteer*

It was a crisp fall afternoon in the early months of the Duneland Resale mission – a time when we early volunteers were feeling our way along, and people were just beginning to discover our shop. I was the cashier that afternoon, and not much was going on.

In truth, I was rather bored, wishing I could be doing something – nearly anything – else. I could be outside walking with a friend and enjoying the beautiful day, raking leaves, reading a good book, or even cleaning house. But, no, I was here, waiting for customers in a shop that was all but empty.

In fact, the only customers were a modestly dressed young couple, who were painstakingly looking through the racks and obviously searching for a bargain. Finally, the husband laid two pairs of slacks on the counter and, soon after, his wife brought up two dresses and several small items. "That's all we're buying today," she said and looked directly at her husband, who quickly nodded in agreement.

As I began to ring up the merchandise, the young woman walked away to browse a bit more, and I saw her husband look in his wallet, then glance nervously at the cash register.

A Miracle in Progress

He leaned closer to me and said, in a near whisper, "Uh, I-I'm sorry, ma'am. I've changed my mind. I really don't want these pants, after all." Quickly, he added, "But, we'll take the dresses and the rest."

Joy was standing nearby and she and I caught each other's eyes for only a moment. I knew we had the same thought. He was short of money, but he did not want to disappoint his wife. *Should I just give him the pants, or not? Do I even have the authority to do that?* Then there was the matter of his pride. I certainly didn't want to embarrass him.

My face must have registered my concern, and Joy's expression told me that she clearly understood. Almost imperceptibly, she nodded *no*. Reluctantly, I put the dresses and small items into a bag and handed it to him. I wanted to cry.

As the couple reached the door, Joy said, "Oh, please – wait a minute. You know, we were just about to mark these items for clearance. The price of all the clothing, including the pants, would be about the same as you just paid. So. . . here, why don't you take the pants, too?"

The man smiled appreciatively and thanked her. She put the pants into his bag, and then the two left.

Neither Joy nor I said a word and I saw the tears in her eyes as I blinked mine away. Then, that little *Aha*! light bulb in my head blinked on. It was

A Miracle in Progress

truly an epiphany. Suddenly, I understood what this Resale mission was all about and what we were doing here.

No matter how small the task, no matter how insignificant it seemed, the work we were doing provided a very necessary service to the community – to people who needed it. And most important – this mission kept people's dignity intact. That was the moment when I truly became a part of Duneland Resale.

ASK, and it will be given you; SEEK, and you will find; KNOCK, and it will be opened to you.
Jesus' words in Matthew 7:7 (RSV)

A Miracle in Progress

A Place Where I Belong

~ *as told by Peggy Dalton, volunteer,*
  to Ann Howard, volunteer

I sat on the bed and stared at the piles of clothing lying all around me. I had cleaned out the closet and the drawers and organized the clothes into neat stacks – undershirts, underpants, ties, socks, shirts, pants, and so on. Reluctantly, but persistently, I had plodded through this task, which had seemed endless.

Since losing my loved one, it was as if I had been living in a dream, with everything happening in slow motion. I knew that it was important to keep myself moving, but I was so very tired and overwhelmed. *What next?* Here it all was, right in front of me – what on earth should I do with it?

I thought over my options. These were such nice clothes – much too nice to be wasted. Someone could surely use them. I felt good about wanting to help others, but this was so difficult. Each piece of clothing held a memory, and it was hard to let go of the memories – these memories of him. Still, I wanted to bring something positive out of my loss.

I picked up his handsome suit jacket and felt the soft fabric. Perhaps a man wanting to look his best for a job interview would like this fine suit. *But who? How would I find him?* I sat for a while,

A Miracle in Progress

puzzled, and then the answer came to me. *Of course...* I knew exactly what to do, and the thought made me smile.

Friends had talked so much about Duneland Resale and how much good it had done – what a difference it had made in the community. I had intended to go there and see what the excitement was about, but for one reason or another, I had never gone. Now I would go. I began loading the suits into the car and, a short while later, pulled into the parking lot and up to the door marked "Donations."

As soon as the car stopped, I began to lose my resolve. These clothes – these memories – were so much a part of me. *Could I actually do* t*his*? I sat there for a moment, not knowing whether to stay, or leave. I felt so alone and there was no one to help me, no one to encourage or discourage me. No, I knew that this was the right thing to do. This was the right time, and I was going to do it . . . now.

In that instant, two men appeared at my car and offered to help me carry in my donation, and then they began unloading the clothes. Their kindness overwhelmed me. Scooping up the remaining armload of suits, I walked through the door and into the back room.

Once inside, I stood there, bewildered, as I looked around the room and wondered what to do now. Then I saw two women walking toward me.

A Miracle in Progress

They were smiling at me. Impossible as it seemed, I knew immediately that, somehow, without my saying a word, they understood. They could sense my distress, my sadness, my aching loneliness. Their arms reached out to enfold me in their warmth. I could feel their love and their genuine concern for me. For the first time, I did not feel alone or afraid. I felt safe, at last.

It was clear to me that I had found a place where I belonged. I told myself, "This is what I want to do – to be here, and work, and give to others what these women have given me." I felt a peace that I had not felt in a long while. I knew that I was home.

After six years of volunteering, Peggy says this: "I love to volunteer at Duneland Resale because being there makes me feel as if I'm with family. Seeing customers' happiness when they come across a great 'find' is exciting to me. I love helping other people. I am so thankful to be at this place where so many people are being helped and where wonderful things – miracles from God – are taking place all of the time."

A Miracle in Progress

Why I Am Here

~ *by Dr. Dan Keilman, volunteer*

Some places and people you cannot stay away from. For me, that place is Duneland Resale and the people are the volunteers.

Seven years ago, I retired as an elementary school principal. I had averaged about seventy hours a week at school. I found that serving families by assisting their children as they learn can be the greatest thrill of a lifetime.

Immediately after I retired, I found myself flirting with depression. What was I going to do to make my time meaningful? A life of sports, reading, cooking, visiting, gardening – waiting for something truly fulfilling to happen – became a nightmare. These were not the days of leisure of which I had dreamed.

Things could not get worse, or could they? I started to look for things to improve our home, yard, and garden. Painting, carpentering, even some minor plumbing and electrical projects became a welcome distraction for a while. For a while! Then they became a nightmare. I found that I could paint, but do very little else when it came to house repairs, garden, and yard work. We soon had six months of messes prevailing inside and outside our home. "Begun, but not completed," became a mantra.

A Miracle in Progress

This period ended when the State Department of Education offered me a position at its offices in Indianapolis. This was work I could do, even complete. Although I loved my work and the people at the Department of Education, I was not home, except on weekends. Being away from those you love most can lead to loneliness. Being away from a great community has the same impact. After three and a half years at the Department of Education, I considered returning and joining fully in life in Duneland.

While I was in Indianapolis, I read the *Chesterton Tribune* every day. Something special drew me to stories about this new resale shop in town. It seemed consistent with the loving, caring nature of Duneland. The shop's natural and supernatural connection with the commandment to love our neighbors as ourselves, and doing what we can for the least of our brothers and sisters, caught my imagination.

When I returned to town, I began to talk to Dan and Joy Johnston and many others in Resale who had been captured by the call to serve their community. I regretted that I did not have time to get involved in what I perceived to be a "foretaste of Heaven." I informed the resalers that I would work if there were special needs. The ever alert Dan soon found these "special needs." The rest is history.

A Miracle in Progress

I was immediately impressed by those giving many more hours at the shop than I felt I could. I soon found out many of these volunteers were much busier than I. They saw a need and were determined to address it. During my limited times at the shop, I found many persons possessed by a proactive love of people, especially the needy. I met fantastic persons contributing items and others buying them. I watched a board of directors building miracles for the Duneland community. Contact with all who are part of Resale – donors, buyers, volunteers, servers, caregivers, miracle workers – changes one's heart and soul.

Dan Keilman's busy Resale volunteer life involves more than counseling.

A Miracle in Progress

As a former school counselor, I now offer services to those who ask for help at Duneland Resale. This work is so rewarding! Bringing love to the troubled is the fulfillment of every life dream.

Giving one's love, service, generosity, and commitment to a worthy purpose is an opportunity to be part of a miracle. Spend an hour or a few hours or a day at Duneland Resale, and you will know that there is much more to your life than the miracle you already are.

A Miracle in Progress

Where People Care

~ by Phyllis Bishop, volunteer

I feel so strongly about the amazing volunteer-family at Duneland Resale. On Wednesdays I work with Laurie Ream, who was in rehab at the nursing home last year. When I visited her, she apologized for not being at the shop to sort, price, and straighten "her" baby clothes!

As soon as she was able, she returned to work with us, sitting on her chair and doing her own tasks. One day she brought me an empty Easter basket with a stuffed bunny attached, explaining that her own children had given it to her last year. She thought that perhaps my own elderly mother would like to have it this year. Oh, my! That basket now sits by my 94-year-old mother's chair in her small room in Illinois.

Duneland Resale is a happy place, where workers truly care about each other. We pray for each other's families and share daily joys and sorrows. Each volunteer I've met has a special "story" in my heart – something that each one has said or done that humbles me and uplifts me with the knowledge that God has worked in our lives in so many ways.

A Perfect Fit

~ by Christi Kalbe, volunteer

Being a major tomboy, I grew up always wanting to be a police officer, security guard, and Army Reservist like my dad, who died of cancer when I was 11.

We moved from Ohio to Indiana to be closer to my mom's family and, when I was 16, I joined the Porter Fire Department as a cadet, along with my cousins, Tony and Rob, and my Uncle Peanut. My family had a long history with the department. In fact, my late grandfather had also been a Porter Firefighter, so it seemed a natural thing to do. I absolutely LOVED the fire service and that became my passion.

After graduating from CHS, I tried getting hired at Bethlehem Steel Fire Department, which was run by Burns Security at the time, but they would only hire me as a security guard, telling me there were no positions available on the fire department. I was patient and took a position as a guard, fulfilling ONE of my childhood dreams – to be like my dad. I had worked as a guard for a year at both Worthington Steel and the Orville Redenbacher Popcorn factory, when I was finally given a spot at the mill.

It was like a dream come true for me! I worked every hour they'd give me – 75.5 hours my

A Miracle in Progress

first week! I took every training opportunity, becoming an EMT, Haz-Mat Tech, a Confined Space Rescue team member, and eventually the first female fire officer in the history of the department. I was very proud of that! However, it was not an easy life because I was also raising my son, my most precious gift from Heaven. Between the job and motherhood, I felt completely blessed!

Unfortunately, I was demoted from my officer position because I wrecked the aerial truck, and the new company that took over could not find any record showing I had been trained to drive that vehicle. Of course, one had to be trained to drive EVERY vehicle in order to become an officer in the first place, but logic did not prevail. I was put back out on crew, where I injured myself on a job.

I have a very strong work ethic and had been working through several other injuries. Somehow I was still able to walk and to work, though the pain was increasingly unbearable. At the time I was unaware I had a severed tendon in my ankle.

In January of 2001 the pain had become so severe that I hadn't been able to sleep for weeks, and I contracted an antibiotic-resistant sinus infection. I called off, thinking I would get it fixed and come right back. I did not know I would never be able to return. Later I found out that I have a genetic collagen disorder called Ehlers-Danlos Syndrome, which causes my joints to dislocate constantly, pinch nerves, tear and stretch tendons, and never heal properly. I thought I was being tough by continuing to work through my pain, but I was doing even more damage. I was only 27 years old when I became disabled.

Now I had to figure out how I was going to live the rest of my life. Being unable to work, and not knowing how to do anything but the fire career that I could no longer have, how was I going to raise my son?

I was so stressed that I was having panic attacks. I was depressed. I was afraid. I hadn't been going to church while I was working because I worked so many hours (60-80+ per week), and when I was home I spent as much time as possible with my son. The rest of the time was for sleeping.

I went back to church and joined the choir to encourage my mom, who was stressed, too, and also hadn't been going to church. I hoped that my going would get her going and give her some kind of peace.

There I met our minister at the time, Pastor Ed Mitchell. He was a very humble and genuine person, and I liked him instantly. He had trouble figuring out his computer and, since I'd had some experience using one at the Fire Department, I offered to help. He asked about my other skills and leaned on me for support when he needed something figured out or done quickly. It felt really good to be useful and productive and to feel needed. I began to participate more and more in church activities.

Then Pastor was diagnosed with cancer. He told me that he needed to go in for chemo. He said that he volunteered as a cashier at Duneland Resale Shop and he asked if I could fill in for him on the days of his treatments. Even though I told him that I hadn't used a cash register since working at Taco Bell when I was 16, he said he was confident that I was the right person for the job.

I was very nervous going in, because I'm generally shy and not very good at meeting new people. I learned that the volunteers at Duneland Resale are entirely different, though. There is just something about them. It doesn't take long until they make you feel like family. They make you feel useful and needed, just as Pastor Ed did. They make you feel loved and cared about, and when you have that feeling and faith, too, no problem is too big to overcome!

It took time, but everything in my life turned around. I'm not rich, but I have everything I need; and all of my fears were, of course, unfounded.

I can't imagine how much harder it would have been to go through that experience without Pastor Ed and those at Resale to make me feel like a productive member of society, one who is useful, loved and needed. I am forever indebted to them, and I am dedicated to making sure that others can experience the same feelings that I have.

A Miracle in Progress

Worker Bees

~ *by Phyllis Bishop, volunteer*

It had been another busy day at the Duneland Resale. I felt as if I'd hustled from one end of the shop to another a thousand times, and these old knees were feeling it! Between carrying items onto the sales floor and answering customers' questions, I felt as if I was way behind. As I carried children's clothing toward the racks, I hesitated with dismay. The toy shelves were nearly emptied onto the floor! I moaned, realizing that I'd already cleaned this area at least a dozen times, and now the mess was even worse than before. Depositing the children's clothes in a pile on a nearby rack, I stood, wondering where to begin.

Behind me, three children rushed eagerly down the aisle of the shop toward the array of scattered toys. The children were preschool age, the youngest a little girl with curly blond hair and bright eyes. "Hello there!" I exclaimed. "I surely am happy to see you! Just what I need ... some Worker Bees!"

The little ones stopped in their tracks with puzzled looks, momentarily distracted from the toys all around them.

"You see," I continued, "we have lots of grandmas who come here. They are older and walk

A Miracle in Progress

with canes. I can't leave toys all over the floor, because those grandmas will trip and fall."

By this time, the two older boys were looking a bit disappointed that I was keeping them from playing by talking so much and dismayed by my notion that the toys didn't belong on the floor.

"I bet you don't know what a Worker Bee is," I quickly continued. "A Worker Bee helps to do some work and then gets paid! That Worker Bee can choose one toy, and keep it for free!" I finally had their interest! "So, I'll start picking up all the toys and putting them back on the shelf. If you can help me, you may pick any toy you like and keep it. I'll tell the lady at the cash register and your mommy that you are Worker Bees!"

The tallest boy quietly said, "But we didn't put any toys on the floor."

"Well, Worker Bees just go to work," I replied. With that, I began to pick up toys, replacing them onto the shelves. Without another word, all three children followed suit. It took the four of us at least 15 minutes to restore the corner to order, so I occasionally noted aloud what great Worker Bees I'd found. The little ones encouraged each other and asked where to put things, and they were industrious beyond belief. As we surveyed the newly cleaned area of the rug and the straightened shelves, I reminded the three that they had now earned a free toy, and that I would tell Mommy and the cash register lady.

A Miracle in Progress

The mother was nearby and I quickly thanked her for bringing in such helpful children and explained that each one had earned a free toy of their choosing. I returned to my task of hanging clothing on the rack, stopping to let our cash register volunteer Pat know that the little ones would be choosing a toy.

A few moments later, I was straightening items on the other side of the shop. The young mother approached me tentatively, with the little girl by the hand. "Would it be all right," she asked, "if my daughter picks out a pair of shoes instead? You see, she really wants a pair of red shoes, and shoes are what we needed to find today."

I was overwhelmed by the mother's soft plea and the little one holding that pair of red shoes. Trying hard not to cry, I knelt down to the child's eye level, and said that her shoes would be just fine. "In fact," I told the mother, "your Worker Bees did their jobs so well that they may choose both a toy and a pair of shoes today."

The mother smiled thankfully and hurried back to the shoe area where her boys were waiting. It was clear to me that this small family on a limited budget felt thankful for the gift of badly-needed shoes.

But I was the one who received the real gift that day. I was blessed to realize why our shop exists, and how our Christian volunteers shine their faith in many ways. Scripture came alive for me,

A Miracle in Progress

as the Lord reminded me once again that we must take care of "the least of these," and "when I was naked, you clothed me."

TWO
Earth Angels

~ by Ann Howard, volunteer

In late afternoon on August 19, 2009, a tornado roared through Chesterton and in thirteen minutes damaged 211 buildings. The miracle was that, with all the devastation, not a single person was seriously injured. But there was more. The tornado, on its path along the railroad tracks, ripped off entire roofs and huge sections of roofs, including Duneland Resale's, and left much debris in its wake.

Craig Berg was among those cleaning up the area when they heard the distant whistle of a train. Seeing the rubble heaped on the tracks, they rushed to clear it away before the train came. Moments after they had finished, a train full of passengers sped by, unharmed. That was the second miracle.

Last was the miraculous community response to this disaster. First responders, police and fire departments, as well as many caring citizens, rushed in to help. Local restaurants and neighbors sent food and drink to sustain the workers. These tireless people did what they could

A Miracle in Progress

that evening, and when night fell, some stayed to guard the damaged areas. At daybreak the community was shocked at the full extent of the damage.

Pinney's Court neighborhood was harder hit than most other areas. Many trees were swept into the nearby creek, a number of roofs were blown away, and there was much more damage to homes. Volunteers rallied quickly and organized work groups to help those in distress.

Kevin Nevers, a reporter for the *Chesterton Tribune*, wrote: "Help, however, isn't simply on the way. Help has already arrived, in the form of Christ's hands and feet: a ministerial group of pastors, lay ministers, and other volunteers from churches throughout Porter County. . . sent a contingent to Pinney's Court to begin the work of unblocking the creek."

What a testimony to the generous spirit and cooperation within our community and in our area!

A Miracle in Progress

A Band of Angels

~ *as told by Alice Perney, friend of Resale,
to Ann Howard, volunteer*

There are many Earth Angels within our community. While we are constantly bombarded with negativity and bad news, we have only to look around us or read the local newspapers to find instance after instance of these giving people.

This is the story of not one, but an entire neighborhood of Earth Angels. Florence Poppo of Chesterton is a 93-years-young woman who can frequently be seen riding her three-wheeled bicycle all around our town. Roskoe, her little white fluff-ball of a dog and her constant traveling companion, sits behind her in his basket and proudly surveys the scene. Florence cheerfully nods and greets friends and strangers as Roskoe wags his tail and yips with delight at the various smells, sights, and sounds about him.

"There goes Mrs. Green for her morning coffee at the neighbor's house," he seems to say. "Oh, hello! There's Craig, and now here comes Heather. I think I'll give them a big wag this morning." He wiggles in his basket. "Say, isn't that little Billy peeking out from the side of that garage? Hmmm . . . Shouldn't he be in school today? Oh, oh! There goes old Mr. Gordon,

A Miracle in Progress

running that stop sign again!" He barks and then settles back, basking in the sunshine.

But one late August day, the sunshine went away. On that dark day, Florence and Roskoe's daily excursions came to an abrupt end as a tornado roared and ripped its way through town, leaving a wake of destruction. After the storm passed, when Florence ventured outside to assess the damage, she was horrified to find her bicycle wrapped around a tree. It was ruined and she was devastated.

Her insurance agent offered her very little consolation. Oh, certainly her ruined bike would be replaced – time, perhaps in a month or two. After all, his company was inundated with tornado-related claims, and didn't she know – these things take time? *Time?* Didn't he know that time is precious? It was already late summer. In Indiana, the fall weather is quite unpredictable – sometimes warm and sunny, but often cold, grey, and unbelievably wet. Florence's riding time was quickly slipping away from her, and all she could do was wait.

Florence was quite discouraged, and her neighbors felt her loss as deeply as she did. Her neighbor Alice Perney would look out the window and see Florence standing and staring sadly at her beloved bicycle. Then she would walk over to the broken bike and simply touch it. It was too much to bear.

A Miracle in Progress

Something had to be done. There could be no long wait for the insurance company. Alice and five other neighbors talked. They would find an identical bicycle and buy it for Florence. Determined, they finally found the bicycle in Michigan, and Ken Jaggers volunteered to drive up to get it. They would surprise her on Sunday after church.

The Sunday's sermon about giving to others was particularly moving. As people left church, Alice tearfully whispered to a friend, "I feel as if that sermon was meant just for me. We're giving the bicycle to Florence today, in just a little while, and I can hardly stand it! This morning I saw her go out and touch that broken bicycle again, and I had to bite my tongue to keep from saying, 'Just you wait – a in a few hours you'll have your new bike!' "

Florence Poppo and Roskoe rejoice over their new bike.

A Miracle in Progress

That afternoon with joyful hearts, the neighbors presented Florence and Roskoe with their brand new three-wheeled bicycle.

`Alice said later, "Florence kept looking at that bike and asking, "Is it really mine? Is it really mine?"

There is no doubt these Earth Angels were as happy in the giving as Florence and Roskoe were in the receiving of this gift.

Alice is one of Florence's Earth Angel neighbors. She is a dedicated volunteer in our community, and she spends countless hours and considerable energy to make our Meals on Wheels program such a success.

Florence celebrates her new gift from her generous neighbors.

A Miracle in Progress

A Random Act

~ *by Pat Amstutz, volunteer*

On a bitter cold, dreary November morning at Duneland Resale, I witnessed the work of an Earth Angel. Sales had been steady that morning, when a young woman came up to the cash register and began to unload her purchases, one by one.

As she handed me each item, she made a comment, such as, "I've never had one of these, and I've always wanted one," or, "Isn't this the most beautiful vase you've ever seen?"

By the time the last item was rung up, at least four other customers were waiting. When I told her that the total was sixty dollars, her face immediately fell.

"I don't have that much," she said.

She had a gift certificate for twenty dollars and about ten dollars in cash. I suggested that she choose the items she needed the most, while I checked out other customers at the opposite register. My partner Chris Medley started to unpack the woman's items, and I heard the woman's sighs of sadness as her treasures were laid aside.

I began to check out the next customer when one of my Wednesday regulars, who happened to be third in line, asked me, "How

A Miracle in Progress

much money does she need to buy everything she picked out?"

"Thirty dollars," was my response.

The customer reached into her wallet and handed over that amount, saying that it was an early Christmas present.

As Chris repacked her treasures, the young lady said, "Thank you so much and God bless you."

After the young lady left, I, too, thanked the generous customer, the Earth Angel.

"I have so much that it's only right that I share," she said. "That thirty dollars meant very little to me, but everything to someone else."

A Miracle in Progress

We Are His Hands

~ *by Margo Ulrich, volunteer*

God knows what you need, and He provides it, down to every detail. After I started working at Duneland Resale, a lovely woman befriended me, encouraged me, and even brought me small gifts of gratitude for my volunteering there. One day she told me that her son, who was in his forties, had developed serious medical problems and was moving to Chesterton so that she and her husband could look after him. She was beside herself, not knowing where he would live or how to get the furniture he would need. She did not have answers, but as always, God did.

One day in the shop, not long after our conversation, I overheard the loud speaker: "Margo, there's someone here to see you." It was the woman and her husband. Having found an apartment for their son, they were looking for a computer desk, which they wanted to purchase and then pick up at a later time.

I asked them to excuse me for a moment. Somehow I knew that they wanted more than just a computer desk. They wanted to find some furniture to help their son feel at home. I also knew that there were suitable pieces on the floor: three bookcases, one with a shelf for a television, a comfortable "chair-and-a-half," and also a large

A Miracle in Progress

computer desk. Only two problems remained – cost, and the storage of the furniture until their son could move into the apartment.

I explained the situation and asked Dan Johnston what to do. Without hesitation, he made a rare exception and lowered the price. "What about the late pick-up date?" I asked, knowing that storage space was always a problem for us.

He was silent as he thought over the situation. I could almost read his mind: *We could put the furniture here, or possibly some might fit over ther and some in that corner.* Finally, he said, "Go ahead and tell them we'll keep all of the furniture here until they have a place to put it."

Excited, I flew back to tell them the good news. I pointed out the pieces which I thought they could use and gave them the prices. Then I told them that we would keep the furniture until they could pick it up. "You think it over and I'll be back in a while," I said.

When I returned, the woman was in tears, and said, "You've given us more than we could have ever imagined. The furniture is perfect and we'll be able to afford it. We can't thank you enough!" They were so delighted that they offered to bring me lunch.

"No," I said, "don't thank me. Just thank God. He's the one who, in His way, has provided for your needs." We raised our hands and voices and thanked God for this blessing.

A Miracle in Progress

When we were finished and they had left, I walked into the back room. The first thing that I saw was a ceramic baby Jesus in the manger. The baby's hands had been broken off and needed to be reattached. I wished that we could keep the broken baby Jesus in a place to remind us that we are His hands, helping God to provide what others need. All of us – the volunteers, the people who donate to us, and those who buy our goods – are doing His work.

Margo, a former volunteer who has moved out of the area, was a wonder at managing two of our largest departments, furniture and knick-knacks.

A Miracle in Progress

Just a Small Thing

~ *by Ann Howard, volunteer*

Our volunteers are often reminded that people are our main concern. Every customer wants to be appreciated and treated with dignity. How true!

One afternoon a customer was waiting at the cash register as her purchases were being checked out. Noting that the items were rather bulky, Nona Ong, one of our pleasant and capable cashiers, picked out a large, sturdy plastic bag, but then paused and put it down. She smiled at the lady.

"Say, how about a really pretty shopping bag instead?" she said. Nona chose a lovely, flowered shopping bag and placed the items inside.

The lady looked at the bag, and tears trickled down her cheeks. She smiled back at Nona and said, "How very kind of you. Thank you so much. The world is truly full of miracles, isn't it?" and she left.

Even small unexpected gestures of kindness can bring joy to others.

A Miracle in Progress

People Who Care

*~ as told by a volunteer
to Ann Howard, volunteer*

My husband introduced me to "Jim," who was his childhood neighbor and friend. Suffering from Lupus and ravaged by the disease of alcoholism, Jim was in a wheelchair by the time we met. He was living in a tiny, sparsely furnished apartment and surviving on a small disability income.

Each week when I would go to the grocery store for him, his list was always the same: a case or two of beer, a carton of cigarettes and seven frozen dinners. On these errands, it seemed that I would always run into someone from church or work who would raise a knowing eyebrow at me. Oh, what they must have thought!

Jim was an artist, musician, poet, writer and spiritual seeker who loved nothing more than a long philosophical discussion. He was also a wonder with duct tape. Almost everything he owned was duct-taped together, most noticeably his wheel chair and jacket. He was so proud of his old bomber jacket, and as the worn leather ripped again and again, he would add more tape. It's a wonder that his rickety wheel chair held up as long as it did. Never underestimate the power of duct tape!

A Miracle in Progress

Having been a Resale volunteer and knowing Joy and Dan Johnston well, I was certain they would help Jim. And of course, they did. Hearing about his situation, they told me to pick out any coat at all, and I left with a handsome soft leather bomber jacket with a luxurious warm lining.

They also gave me Joan Knibbs' phone number. Joan, a kind and generous woman, runs the Duneland Medical Equipment Closet and lends medical equipment free of charge to those who need it. Before the sun set on that cold winter day, Jim had a beautiful warm coat and a fine wheel chair. He cried like a small child when he saw them.

Dan and Joy also said to ask what else Jim needed, and he told me that he could use a mattress. He confided that he had been sleeping on a coffee table piled with lumpy old cushions and pushed up against a wall. A short time later Jim had a brand new mattress and box springs that Dan delivered and set up for him.

For the rest of that winter and the chilly days of early spring, Jim looked very handsome in his bomber jacket as he cruised around in his sturdy, dependable wheelchair. He did not live much longer, but for the first time in a long while he looked well rested and peaceful. Jim learned that there are people in this world who truly do care.

A Miracle in Progress

Earth Angels All Around Us

~ by Ann Howard, volunteer

One afternoon Margaret Schoenborn, a friend who periodically comes to Duneland Resale to collect clothing for the prison ministry, looked around at the busy volunteers, and said, "When I come here, I feel as if I'm in a hall of angels."

Of course, we were deeply touched by her remark, but certainly our volunteers do not view themselves as angels. Nevertheless, her comment awakened an awareness of the presence of those Earth Angels about us.

Our volunteers go about quietly doing God's work. Through their service at and their missions beyond the shop, these Resale angels undoubtedly contribute to the creation of small and large miracles in people's lives.

Each month Louise Barrett, who is severely visually impaired, joyfully places the numbers on 1,000 Resale price tags. Several years ago, a woman who was referred to us by the Trustee received our help. For a time she came to scrub the floors and asked for nothing in return.

For a year or more, a group of volunteers gathered together to clean various areas of the shop. Now Donna Brown, our "purse lady," among

A Miracle in Progress

her other talents, also scrubs our bathrooms and more.

Maurice Trimble, who has now passed away, gathered, cleaned, sorted and packaged over 10,000 golf balls for the shop. In addition, he and Craig Holman regularly drove from Valparaiso to Resale to haul away our cardboard for recycling.

Bob Taylor, our "lamp man," repaired many lamps for us and always enjoyed visiting with the volunteers. He also donated an eye-catching "leg lamp," complete with fishnet stocking, to Resale.

Recently Joy related a story which further exemplifies behavior typical of the character and ethics of our volunteers. Pat McDonald, while tagging clothing, found $25 in the pocket of a garment and immediately brought it to the cashier for our donations jar.

"If this occurrence has happened once, it has happened at least 25 times," Joy said. She added that our customers have also found money in pockets of our clothing and brought it to us.

Dr. Dan Keilman, a former administrator in the Duneland school system, is a legend in the community because of his compassion for others. He has made a positive influence in many lives and continues to do so in his work as a volunteer and counselor for Duneland Resale.

Through Kay Johnson, who is one of our busiest Earth Angels, Duneland Resale has reached out to at least eleven or more other organizations.

A Miracle in Progress

Her missions include: Operation Christmas Child, Buckner, Gleam, Every Child Ministries, the Ernie Mason Family, Pacific Garden Mission, Memorial Christian Hospital and Heart House, Jim and Jan Mulvihill Missionaries, the Baptist Children's Home, Reuz Station for Arts and Crafts Environmental Education Center for use by non-profit organizations, and the Northwest Indiana Women's Center.

She delivers baby items and packages of diapers from Resale to an area pregnancy center as an incentive for women to attend new mothers' classes there.

She takes our reusable craft items to an environmental education center where the items are weighed and reported to the government to show how much was saved from going into landfills. These donations help that organization as well as fulfilling our mission of recycling.

Both Lil and Chuck Swickard have had a long history of volunteerism and leadership, their caring and sharing in the community.

Chuck has been a leader in the Boy Scout program and both he and Lil have had various leadership roles in their church, as have many of our volunteers.

A Miracle in Progress

Chuck Swickard presents a donation to the Boy Scouts.

The list goes on. Alice and Jack Zink and Joan Sitar spend many hours volunteering at the Michigan City Overnight Shelter.

Bill Ong, who has volunteered weekly since the shop's earliest days and also serves as Resale's Treasurer, is on the Board of the Salvation Army. His wife Nona, who has brought her retail experience to the shop, has been a dedicated cashier and our dolls chairman since the beginning. She is a faithful volunteer for Meals on Wheels.

John Komenas has worked on Habitat for Humanity. Christi Kalbe has not only donated her hair to Locks of Love, but she has also used that

A Miracle in Progress

activity to generate funds for our Relay for Life team.

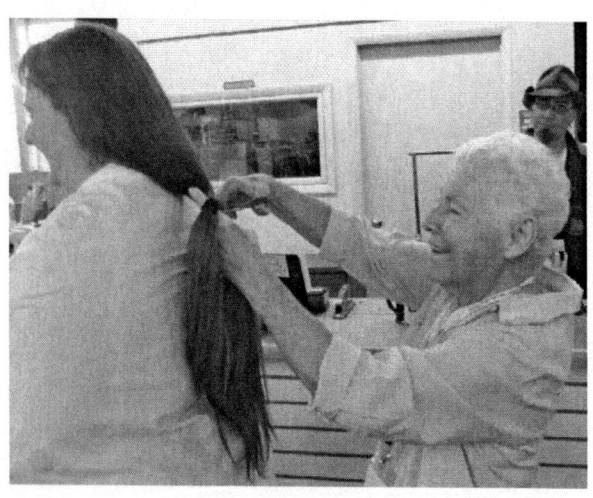

Joan Sitar (right) cuts Christi Kalbe's Locks of Love.

Zella and Roy Olson are leaders in the Friends of the Dunes organization, and Zella has spent much time volunteering at the National Lakeshore. These volunteers, as well as other Resale volunteers, have worked tirelessly to preserve our lovely parks and our environment.

JoAnn, who has passed away, and Bob Ruppenkamp have donated time, kindness and energy to benefit those in need at Resale as well as elsewhere. Bob and Dan Johnston regularly take Resale's extra bicycles to the prison in Michigan City, where inmates rehabilitate them. The prison then donates them to the Boys and Girls Club and those in need.

A Miracle in Progress

In addition to the Resale mission, many of our volunteers are involved in foreign missions. After the Tsunami, Kim Goldak worked with Habitat for Humanity to build a home for an elderly woman in Thailand. Several of the volunteers and their families have sponsored individuals and families in foreign lands. Resale funds have also sponsored a senior citizen in India.

Joy and Dan Johnston have made medical mission trips to Kenya and to the Ukraine. Through the years Dan has made trips to Zambia to work on a clean water project. He designed and planned, pipe by pipe, a system to bring clean water and sanitation to a hospital as well as many buildings in that area.

Chris Medley, who multi-tasks at Resale in her quiet, efficient way, has worked on missions for Native Americans in Sholow and Globe, Arizona.

Of course, this list is far from complete. Our volunteers, modest by nature, do not have much to say about themselves – their service elsewhere, or their accomplishments. We have gleaned what we can, where we can, to give the reader some idea of the generosity of spirit and the humanitarian efforts of volunteers at Duneland Resale. Many have received awards for their volunteerism and community service and we are very proud of them.

For so many reasons, we consider our volunteers Earth Angels

THREE
Miracles of Healing

Our volunteers and customers share miracles experienced in their own lives as well as those at Duneland Resale.

God-Connections

~ by Ann Howard, volunteer

John Clark, who lives in Fort Wayne, Indiana, is the relative of one of our volunteers. One day he was in the Arizona airport, killing time and drinking a beer with a man he had just met after their flight to Chicago was delayed. The man, an urologist, was also continuing on to Fort Wayne.

Somehow, the conversation led to John's talking about his having night sweats. Fortunately for John, the urologist's specialty was kidneys. He told John that night sweats signal that something is wrong with a man's body and that the body is trying to fight the problem by sweating. Urging John to waste no time in checking into his problem, the doctor then offered to test him at his office as soon as they returned.

A Miracle in Progress

The news was bad. The scan showed a cancerous tumor on John's kidney. The growth, however, was still undetectable, not yet large enough to cause other symptoms. Kidney cancer, an insidious disease, does not normally exhibit symptoms until it has metastasized. Now for the good news . . . John's surgery and treatment were successful and today he is cancer-free.

This meeting with a stranger, who happened to be an urologist, who happened to specialize in kidneys, who happened to be going to Fort Wayne, and who helped John get the right test to diagnose his cancer, saved John's life.

This sequence of events was miraculous indeed, and the doctor who helped John is undoubtedly an Earth Angel. Barb, John's wife, said John is a living gift and their entire family is very grateful that God was not yet ready for him.

A Miracle in Progress

The Roller Coaster

~ *by Paula Stolk, friend of Resale*

Bill and I met at a wedding in early July when we were college students at different universities. Our meeting was a set up, but Bill didn't know it. We sat at the same table and thoroughly enjoyed each other's company. While driving me home, Bill asked me for a date, and so began our courtship.

We were a couple until shortly before graduation when we broke up. It was the Viet Nam era, and Bill went into the Army. I went to graduate school, then met and married someone else. Bill, however, was not to be discouraged. Years later, when we finally got together, he said he figured that I'd eventually come to my senses and marry him. That I did.

Bill and I were in love, we were happy, and we were ready for the most thrilling ride of our lives. This is the story of that roller coaster ride, full of excitement and dangers, that has been our life together.

The car started off very slowly, steadily climbing, until it reached the top of the hill. Here, we paused to marvel at the view of our future, which was spectacular. Life held such promise and the tracks ahead looked straight and smooth.

Suddenly, without warning, we hit the first bump, when, in May, Bill was diagnosed with

A Miracle in Progress

colon cancer. We lurched, then headed downward, gaining momentum with every curve. After his surgery in July, the doctor told us that the tumor had penetrated Bill's bowel wall and spread to his lymph nodes. He estimated that Bill had only a 25 percent chance of surviving the year. We were devastated.

Several days later, however, lab reports indicated that the cancer was not in the lymph nodes after all, and the doctor recommended chemotherapy. As Bill went through the months and months of chemotherapy and its side effects, we both felt lost and helpless, unable to see what lay ahead.

Now was the time to grab the handrail and tighten the seatbelts. I enlisted every friend, every acquaintance to pray for him. When the treatments finally ended, the doctor told us that Bill was in remission. Breathing more easily, we settled back to enjoy the ride, unaware of the dangers which lurked around the next curves.

Within the next two years, Bill found two more lumps and the doctor recommended more chemotherapy. We sought a second opinion at the University of Chicago Hospital. Three different doctors informed us the cancer had metastasized and Bill was terminal.

We were at a loss. The car jolted to a stop, and we sat, idling on the track. *What could we do?* They advised us to return to our medical center in

A Miracle in Progress

the south suburbs and follow whatever course those doctors advised. On the way home, Bill said, "I think I should apply for Social Security Disability." He was immediately approved.

Thus started our long and difficult journey of treatments and prayers. Now we were moving again, but the track was rougher than before. Bill ran the gambit of treatments – chemo, oral medications, radiation – each day for a month.

We held on as tightly as we could, and all the while morning prayers, church prayers, and my own desperate prayers swirled around him. Finally, we were told that there were no other treatments available and that we should try elsewhere. *But where?* Now we seemed to be freefalling, caught in a dark, downward spiral.

There were occasional glimpses of light as we learned of new possibilities. We applied for Northwestern Hospital's experimental treatments, but Bill was denied. Next the doctors tried a new form of chemotherapy, using a port that was put into his shoulder to inject chemicals continuously. Then another hard bump rocked us. The tumors were still growing. We prayed and fought to hold on tightly as one sharp turn after another threw us off balance. This ride was too wild, too frightening. I wanted to get off!

But there was no turning back. From Northwestern, we went back to the University of Chicago to see if another kind of treatment was

A Miracle in Progress

possible. The tests revealed that the tumors had grown even larger and were pressing on Bill's organs. The free fall seemed endless. We prayed for a miracle.

When our doctor asked if we had ever considered surgery, we said that we had not and that twelve doctors had refused to operate because they felt Bill would not be able to heal. Then our doctor asked if we had seen an oncology surgeon; we had not. Immediately, he made an appointment with a Dr. Possner, who said that *yes,* he would operate on Bill and that a plastic surgeon would also be there in surgery.

Now we were on the straightaway again, and we strained to catch the elusive glimmers of hope along our way. The surgery took two and a half hours, the closing took five and a half, and the incision took four months to heal. It was a long, arduous process, but at last Bill was getting better.

We were relieved and happy until we hit another bump on the track. Bill found a small lump and back we went to our doctor. Again he performed surgery, this time less invasive. As the necessary check-ups, MRIs, and colonoscopies followed, we sat idly on the track and prayed. We were in limbo.

For five years there were no signs of tumors. The darkness had gradually lifted, and we began inching our way along, cautiously moving upward toward the top. Then an MRI revealed a spot on

A Miracle in Progress

Bill's liver, and we froze. *Please, not again,* we prayed, holding our breath as we waited. It was a false alarm. We exhaled. Our prayers were answered and we were so thankful.

After another year, the doctor announced that Bill was cured. And from that day to this, we have enjoyed the ride as never before. It is by the Grace of God and countless prayers that Bill is with us today. His recovery has been a true miracle.

After that tumultuous first eleven years of our ride, Bill is now in good health. Soon we will have been happily married for 32 years. He has supported me through two Master's Degree programs so that I could have the career I had always dreamed of – that of helping handicapped children in the educational system.

A Miracle in Progress

Turning Point

~ *by Dr. Dan Keilman, volunteer*

Some months ago I learned that Vickii Brock, a friend and a strong community leader, had only one day to live. She was in a local Intensive Care Unit, where an invasive infection had permeated her lungs and kidneys. Her husband Ken and the immediate family were gathered at her bedside, awaiting the devastating inevitability.

I was and am very close to Vickii and her family, but I could not, of course, enter the ICU because I was not a family member. Aware of what was happening, I decided to go to the hospital where I could spend some time visiting with the family members.

Before going, I called the waiting room to make certain they were there. Vickii's daughter Michael Anne answered the phone. I knew that her family was a family of faith and prayer. It was hard for the two of us to speak, but I asked if her mother had received the Anointing of the Sick. She said she had been working to find a priest, but had been unsuccessful so far. I assured her that I would have a priest there within the next half hour.

I am not sure why I made this promise, but somehow God told me that this would be possible if I but made a call to a priest. So then I called a priest who, at that moment, was about ten minutes

A Miracle in Progress

from the hospital. He promised to leave right away and within ten minutes, he was in the ICU.

Vickii was in a typical emotional state for a person in her condition. She was confused and not sure she wanted the Anointing. After all, many people consider the Anointing of the Sick only for those who are critically ill or dying!

Then the priest began to pray with Vickii and she quickly yielded to his request to anoint her. After receiving the anointing, she immediately fell asleep.

Previously she had not slept for days, but now she slept for eleven straight hours. She hardly recognized people or places before this long sleep. As she awoke, the first thing she did was turn to Michael Anne and ask how things were going.

How were things going? Radical changes had occurred in Vickii! Within days, she was out of the hospital and soon after began to resume her normal activities. Today she is again very involved in the community. She recognizes the miracle which brought her back to her style of gracious living and giving.

A Miracle in Progress

An Unexpected Angel

After hearing this story, Pat Amstutz felt that it should be included in our book. Then she asked those involved – Jerry Ward, Duneland Resale electrician and volunteer, and Pastor Cathy Allison, Associate Pastor of First United Methodist Church of Chesterton – to tell about their chance meeting that only God could have arranged.

~ *by Jerry Ward, volunteer*

I must have been a sad sight that day. Having had major neck surgery about two weeks before and wearing a neck collar and a chest harness, I was not feeling my best. While standing in line at the doctor's office in Valparaiso to get an order for a lab test, I noticed a man wearing a Chesterton Fire Department tee shirt directly in front of me.

When I went across the parking lot to the lab, which was full of people, I saw that same man. I signed up for the test, then sat down in the empty seat, which he had just left. I began talking to the woman next to me, who turned out to be his wife. I told her about my problems, neck pain and numbness in my hand and fingers, and the surgeries that followed. She seemed interested in knowing I had gone to Northwestern Hospital, where the doctors found the problem in my neck,

A Miracle in Progress

and in particular, that Dr. Wellington Hsu had performed my surgery.

Her husband came back inside and we began talking about my symptoms. He had experienced similar problems, but so far the doctors had not been able to help him. Then I told him about the Northwestern Ortho Surgery Department and what they had done for me. That afternoon he called me and asked for more information and doctors' names and phone numbers at Northwestern.

Today people tell my wife Betty and me what a remarkable difference our meeting that day has made in Bob's life, and Bob and his wife Cathy have also said how grateful they are that we crossed paths. It's amazing! There I was, simply telling my story – it all just happened that way.

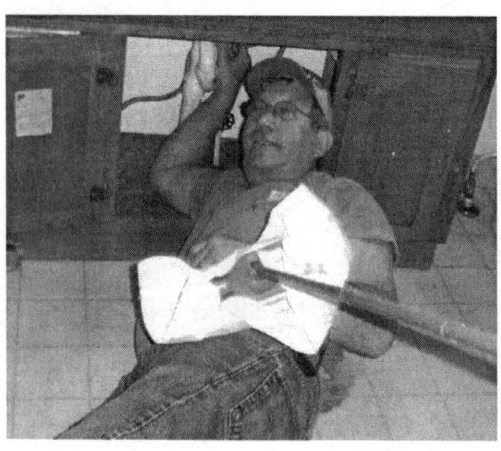

Jerry Ward, a man of all trades, is one of Resale's hardest working volunteers.

A Miracle in Progress

An Unexpected Angel continues

~ by Pastor Cathy Allison, friend of Resale

I always knew that God sends us angels, but I never knew how they would look. God can surprise you!

One day in late April my husband Bob was having a three-hour blood test. Being in constant pain, he had been unable to work for months. The year before he had had an unsuccessful fusion done in the front of his neck, and we were starting to lose hope that he would ever be pain free again.

We had already been at the lab for two hours and at last were in the home stretch. We had talked to everyone in the packed waiting room, but by this time it was quiet. When Bob went to sit on the bench just outside the door, I stayed inside.

Just then an unhappy looking man walked in. He had a combination back and neck brace and he was unable to turn his head from side to side. He checked in, then sat down in the only seat left in the entire room, the one right next to me. My first thought was to join Bob outside because I didn't think I could endure talking to one more unhappy person that day. However, something told me to stay there and, against my better judgment, I stayed.

When the man started talking, looking straight ahead, I wasn't even sure that he was

A Miracle in Progress

talking to me. He said something to the effect that this is what happens when your body – basically your spine – starts to deteriorate. Somehow I assumed that he was in that brace permanently. I was certain that I didn't want Bob talking to him and getting more discouraged, fearful he would end up in the same shape. But I kept listening.

Next the man said that shortly he would be out of his back brace, and after that, the neck brace. I really tuned in to him then. He explained how he had reached this point, basically traveling the same road as Bob, except that his condition obviously had been much worse. He told about Dr. Hsu and his surgery at Northwestern. I was intrigued and let him do all the talking; at that point we hadn't even introduced ourselves.

Bob came back. Before I realized what I was doing, I blurted out that he really needed to talk to this man and I began rambling on about his story. We introduced ourselves to Jerry and continued talking nonstop.

Bob told Jerry about our friend from church who had told us about a friend of hers who had a successful spinal fusion at Northwestern. Jerry asked who had told us the story, and Bob told her that it was Cathy Fitzmaurice.

Grinning, Jerry said, "Don't listen to that lady – she's nuts!"

It turns out that Cathy is a mutual friend of ours and that Jerry was "that guy," the one she had

A Miracle in Progress

told us about when she had given us Dr. Hsu's business card. At that time we did not believe that seeing Dr. Hsu would help. We should have listened to Cathy!

Jerry and Bob exchanged phone numbers and talked even more on the phone that day. Bob contacted Dr. Hsu and made an appointment for the following week. Jerry offered to drive us back and forth to Chicago, even on the day of surgery, which was scheduled for May 18th. He was willing to help us in any way he could.

Not having been able to work since November, Bob had managed to struggle through the "long haul," but after his surgery, he went back to work in August, only two months later.

You never know whom God is going to send your way.

A Miracle in Progress

Fred Wright

~ *by Pat Wright, volunteer*

When Pat heard about the accounts of healing miracles in this book, she was enthusiastic and offered to share two stories of divine intervention experienced by her family. This story is about Pat's son Fred.

In the final days of a biting cold December, Fred, then ten and a half years old, and our younger sons trudged into the house after playing in the snow. The young boys shivered as they peeled off their icy coats, but Fred said he was not cold; instead, he felt very hot and tired. Alarmed to find that he had a very high fever, my husband Harold and I immediately took him to the family doctor.

After examining him, the doctor said, "Fred has bronchitis. I'm prescribing this medicine for him, and it should make him good as new."

In no time Fred was well enough to return to school, but after a few days he again became ill. We took him back to the doctor, who assured us that the boy's symptoms were merely a carryover from bronchitis.

Not long after seeing the doctor, Fred fainted and was rushed to the hospital. Tests indicated internal bleeding, and the doctor now said that the boy obviously had a bleeding ulcer.

A Miracle in Progress

He put Fred on a bland diet of milk, pudding and gelatin and ordered antibiotics, iron shots, and daily transfusions for him. Still Fred's blood count remained dangerously low, and his other troubling symptoms persisted.

We prayed constantly and asked others to join us in prayers for our son's recovery. Seeing no improvement in his condition, we became frantic.

We called in another doctor, who in turn consulted a pediatrician. Harold and I were surprised by the doctors' actions, for in those days general practitioners treated every ailment and rarely called upon other doctors. We were shocked when the pediatrician then called upon a surgeon to assist in the case, and finally, several more pediatricians and surgeons were brought in for consultation. Next the surgeon informed us that the doctors had all agreed that exploratory surgery was necessary for Fred.

The surgery took hours, and our family patiently and prayerfully endured the long wait. At last the surgeon appeared. With his head bowed, he told us that the doctors had looked everywhere possible during the extensive surgery, but had found that Fred no longer had any sign of bleeding or any other signs of illness. Still hoping to find answers, the doctors were sending tissue samples to a laboratory in California.

Within days, even though Fred was still receiving transfusions and exhibiting all the same

A Miracle in Progress

symptoms, he was discharged from the hospital. We waited and waited, but no answers came. Our family prayed even harder than before.

What on earth should we do now? We considered taking Fred to Mayo Clinic where the doctors might be able to help him. *But was the boy strong enough to make the trip? Obviously he was not getting any better, and time was running out. Something needed to be done.* We decided that we should take him to Mayo Clinic and immediately began preparing for the trip.

Then the unexpected happened. The next morning when Fred came downstairs, we noticed a dramatic change in him. His color had markedly improved and he was smiling. We took him back to the doctor, who again ran tests. This time the tests showed was no indication of bleeding or any other signs of illness.

"We have no idea what made Fred ill," the doctor said, shaking his head, "but there is no doubt that the boy is cured. He belongs in the record books!"

Harold and I knew that we had witnessed a miracle. God, through his mercy and grace, had answered prayers and saved our boy from death.

Fred Wright had no recurrence of that mysterious illness and he died at the age of 50 from an unrelated incident.

A Miracle in Progress

Mary Ann Wright

~ by Pat Wright, volunteer

Our volunteer Pat continues her sharing of miracles with this story about her mother, Mary Ann Wright.

In 1897 Mary Ann Wright, one of eleven children, was born in a small Iowa coal mining town called Muchakinock or "bad crossing." The town was so named because rainstorms often turned the gentle river that ran beside it into a raging torrent which through the years had claimed many lives.

During this time because the mines were unsanitary and there were no sewers, diseases swept mercilessly through the densely populated mining communities. Few who lived in these towns survived past the age of forty. Respiratory diphtheria, which causes a membrane to block the airway, was ravaging Muchakinock, and many townspeople had already died.

Mary Ann had contracted the disease and was struggling to breathe. It was obvious to her family that the child was too weak to survive much longer. Her distraught parents called upon the church elders, who came to the house to join the family in praying over her.

A Miracle in Progress

They were in the midst of their prayers when Mary began a violent and lengthy coughing bout which frightened those around her. Suddenly she coughed up a mass which her mother picked up and threw into the coal-burning stove. Afterward, Mary began to breathe more easily, and she showed signs of recovery. Those present were awed by the startling transformation in the child.

When the doctor was called to the house and heard the elders' account of Mary's coughing bout and her miraculous recovery, he was stunned. All those who had been present knew that Mary had been healed through prayer and the Grace of God.

Mary lived on to the age of 82. Pat heard her mother tell this story many times, and she has read the written account of Mary's illness and divine healing in a book of miracles published by a church. Pat says: "God, in saving Mary, gave me a wonderful, loving mother. God has been so very good to our family!"

A Miracle in Progress

The Miracle of Gary

~ as told by Joy and Dan Johnston, volunteers,
to Ann Howard, volunteer

Gary Bennett is a special friend of those at Resale; his story will amaze you. Joy and Dan Johnston first noticed him riding all around town on his bicycle, pulling a bike trailer behind. They could not have missed him. Even in the coldest weather, he seemed to be everywhere, pedaling as fast as he could, his trailer overflowing with various treasures.

"There's that guy, again," they would say.

There's that guy, Gary Bennett!

They were impressed by Gary's persistence, but they were also concerned about him. They had learned that previously he had lived in a boarding house in town, but had been evicted because his loud and uncontrollable yelling was intolerable to the other tenants. When Gary did not take his medication, and often he failed to take it, his inappropriate behaviors alarmed others, and thus made him inadmissible to group homes or shelters.

After leaving the boarding house, he moved into his brother's lease-back home in the Dunes, but only temporarily. Soon his brother moved out of the area and Gary was homeless. By now, Joy and Dan had befriended him, and they were determined to find a suitable home for him.

One of the local churches, as a mission, maintained a house for people in transition from shelters to regular housing. That house, now vacant, was eventually scheduled to be torn down to make space for a church expansion. Though not optimistic, Dan and Joy met with the Mission Committee to see whether they would allow Gary to rent the house for as long a time as it was available.

As they expected, the committee questioned Gary's ability to manage his life while living alone. Dan and Joy admitted that at times his behavior was erratic, but they felt that, with help, he could manage. Furthermore, they pledged to watch over him and make certain that he took his medication and kept up the property.

A Miracle in Progress

Then an unexpected complication arose. They were shocked when Howard Christofersen, a bearded, elderly gentleman, whom they had not met before, came forward, saying he also had come to the meeting in hopes of renting the house for six to eight months. Both Joy and Dan's spirits plummeted, because they felt certain that the committee would consider Howard, who was obviously independent and able-bodied, a more desirable tenant than Gary.

At that point Howard stunned everyone by saying, "Of course, I would be honored to share the house with Gary."

"I'm really sorry to say this. . . I'm afraid that won't work," Dan said. "You need to know that Gary is schizophrenic."

"Well," Howard said, "Actually I am a physician, and I'm familiar with schizophrenia."

"No, really, it just wouldn't work," Dan said. "He yells at times and his actions would surely disturb you."

"No, they definitely would not. I was in charge of the mental ward of a hospital for years. He wouldn't bother me at all," Howard calmly responded.

Dan said, "Excuse me, please. I think my jaw just fell down on my chest! You're a doctor, familiar with schizophrenia, once in charge of a hospital mental ward and you really want to live with Gary? Do I have all this right?"

A Miracle in Progress

"Yes, you do. You have it exactly right," Howard said.

Later, Dan said he and Joy were tempted to look down and see if this man was wearing sandals. He was so much like Jesus! The mission committee agreed to rent the house to both men. As they left, Dan and Joy began to have some doubts. *Was this man serious? Is he really a doctor? Is he crazy? How could all of these unlikely and unbelievable circumstances come together for such a positive outcome?*

There is the saying that if something seems too good to be true, it probably isn't. In this case, however, it was good, and it was true. There was no doubt that Joy and Dan had witnessed a miracle in the coming of Howard.

In the months following, they visited Gary frequently and made certain that he was eating well and that he took his medication on schedule. In addition, Howard seemed to be a stabilizing influence on him. Everyone saw a dramatic improvement in Gary's appearance and in his behavior. He took pride in his clothing and appearance, he held down several jobs and, eventually, he began driving a car. Behind the wheel, he was the master of the universe.

At Halloween, Dan and Joy helped Gary decorate the house. Dressed in costume, he was more excited and happy than the trick-or-treaters, as he handed out generous handfuls of candy to

A Miracle in Progress

them and urged them to take more. He was a child again and he said that he was having more fun than he had ever had. Gary's transformation was the second miracle in his life.

When Howard moved out of the house, Joy and Dan's faithful supervision and friendship enabled Gary to live alone. He came to Resale for his daily medication, he ate well and he thrived. Life for Gary had never been better. And then, without warning, the "other shoe" fell.

One weekend Gary became ill. Joy and Dan took him to the emergency room. The doctor there ordered an X-ray, which revealed a peach-sized mass in Gary's lung. Feeling that a second diagnosis was necessary, Joy and Dan took him to another doctor, who ordered a biopsy which confirmed that indeed there was a large mass. Immediately, that doctor scheduled a meeting with a surgeon. Because Gary is a chain smoker, the medical staff all agreed that the mass was most likely a malignant one. A week before surgery, the surgeon ordered one more X-ray, which confirmed the previous findings.

Joy and Dan's day began at 4:30 a.m. on the morning of the surgery. They left early to help Gary prepare for his 6:00 a.m. arrival at the hospital. Gary was understandably nervous. Joy accompanied him to his bedside while Dan stayed in the waiting room.

A Miracle in Progress

The ER nurse came to talk to Gary and said, "I want to prepare you. This is what's going to happen to you. After the surgery, when you awaken, you will be in the Intensive Care Unit. You will not be able to speak because there will be many tubes coming out of your body."

Gary, who had been nervous before, was now petrified. The doctor then informed Joy and Gary that he had ordered one final X-ray to make certain that nothing had changed. Then Gary was wheeled out of the room. He was brought back soon after.

Since only one person at a time could be in his room, Joy and Dan took turns staying with him, and they tried, without success, to calm him. Joy was with him when finally he was given medication to relax him in preparation for the anesthesia.

A short while later Dan, sitting in the waiting room, suddenly looked up to see Joy, sobbing, as she approached him. "Y-you'll never believe what just h-happened," she managed to say.

Then she told him this unbelievable story:

As Gary was on the gurney and being wheeled down the hall to surgery, the surgeon rushed out, and said, "Stop right now! I won't be operating on this man." Amid gasps of surprise, he said to the nursing staff, "The new X-ray clearly

A Miracle in Progress

shows that all is clear. There is absolutely nothing in this man's lung. The surgery is canceled."

Later that day after Gary was released from the hospital, he visited his neighbor, Reverend Terry Rhine, the Methodist Minister, who along with many others had been praying for him. "They say I'm a miracle," Gary announced, as the puzzled minister, not yet knowing what had happened, tried "to connect the dots."

"Well, said the minister, "you know, many of us have been praying for you, Gary."

Gary smiled, and said,"Oh, you church people! I know you and your prayers helped me!"

A month later, to make certain that the mass was gone, Gary went back to the hospital for another X-ray. Again, it was clear. And this was Gary's third miracle. Thanks be to God.

FOUR
Glimpses of God

Miraculous Moments

~ as told by volunteers
to Ann Howard, volunteer

Psalm 37:4: "Delight thyself also in the Lord; and he shall give thee the desires of thine heart."

Kay Johnson expressed these thoughts about the miracles, the gifts from God, at Duneland Resale. "Just as God is concerned about the birds of the air and lilies of the field, He is also interested in meeting our individual needs and desires as we read in Matthew 6:25-34. He is concerned with little, insignificant gifts, as well as the larger needs in our life."

Volunteers are repeatedly amazed by these moments. The frequency of these occurrences is proof to us that they are not merely coincidences. An unknown author defines coincidence in this way: "Coincidence is when God chooses to remain anonymous." Here are examples of some inspiring "glimpses of God" at Resale.

In the very early days of Resale, Roy Brush was tirelessly arranging clothing on a diminishing

A Miracle in Progress

supply of hangers. "What we really need here are more hangers," he said. Soon after, the local Ben Franklin, which was closing, brought in more hangers than we could use.

    Judy Ross said that she needed plastic Easter eggs for an upcoming celebration at the shop. Since Easter was long past, she wondered where she could find them. Right then, another volunteer brought her a box of plastic Easter eggs that had just been donated. Much later Judy again needed Easter eggs which were, as before, out of season; soon after, a bag of them was donated.

    Next, she needed dog-related items for our Bark for Life fundraiser for the American Cancer Society. You may not be surprised to learn that in one day three dog sweatshirts and several other dog items were donated. Much to our delight, we soon had more dog items than we could use.

    Peggy Dalton was having a bad day. She was trying to tag and hang clothing on the racks, but her back was hurting. She commented that she could really use a back support. Another volunteer instantly produced one that had been donated.

    Carol Sterken, a former volunteer and a frequent shopper at Resale, had exhausted herself searching in various stores for a travel purse, one with zippers and pockets, for an upcoming trip. Those she had already seen were too large, too small, or too expensive, and she was discouraged. Soon she would be leaving. When she came in to

A Miracle in Progress

work her shift, she was astonished. There it was – the purse she had been seeking! It had all the necessary nooks and pockets, it looked brand new, and the price was right.

Next she found a set of glasses which matched a set of dishes she had purchased elsewhere the year before. She still marvels at another find – a small sewing cabinet with several drawers – exactly what she needed!

Dan Johnston announced our desperate need for dusk-to-dawn lights. Within a few days, a woman donated three of them to us. Several years later, in order to get necessary construction permits for the building we were purchasing to house our new facility, he needed blueprints. Unfortunately, the sellers had none.

Next he checked with an architectural firm and learned that the estimated the cost of making new ones was $3500 to $4000. Being ever-thrifty and extremely determined, Dan again talked to the sellers, who suggested that he call the original builders, a local construction firm. The news there was not good. The woman in charge said that there were prints available, but that half of them were too dark to read. She wondered if they were even worth copying.

"That's okay," Dan said. "Half is better than none. Please go ahead and copy them and we'll see what we can do with them."

A Miracle in Progress

Soon after, she called Dan to say that she had found an entire set of blueprints for the building, and furthermore, the prints were in perfect condition. She said, "I can't imagine where they came from. I had thoroughly searched that cabinet for the prints and found only the one set. When I opened that drawer this morning, there they were. It's unbelievable!"

Kay Johnson needed a bell to help her find her dog, which kept running away. Before the day was over, the bell appeared. Recently she wrote: "Last week my husband said he needed a new umbrella to keep in his car. He asked me to look for one at the Resale shop. 'But,' he said, 'I want a black one!' Lo and behold, on Tuesday when I went to work, a black one came in. I purchased it for $1.00. Ask and ye shall receive!"

Brandon Fero, the son and grandson of Resale volunteers, returned from several tours in Iraq. We had just begun a welcome home celebration with cake and balloons, when much to our surprise, representatives from a local restaurant walked in with a gift for us – four submarine sandwiches. Perfect timing!

Ray Tamborski, who was one of our back door volunteers, is an avid Chicago Blackhawks fan. He frequently wore his team shirt and hat. Moments before we gathered in the kitchen to celebrate his fiftieth birthday, in came a tailor-made donation – a souvenir Blackhawks hockey stick. Linda Handlon said that the sight of this perfectly timed and most apropos donation gave her goose bumps.

Kay said, "Many times people have entered Duneland Resale expressing a need or desire for something and at just that time or soon after, a donation arrives that meets their need."

For quite a while Dana, one of our customers, had been fruitlessly looking for white scrubs, and specifically white scrub pants. While shopping at Resale one day, she found unexpected treasures – not one, but five pairs of white scrub pants in her size. She was ecstatic as she brought them to the cashier and shared her story.

Margaret Schoenborn came to pick up the clothing Joy had set aside for her prison ministry. She was amazed that the sizes were exactly what she needed.

As Michelle Thompson came to pick up a check for the Girl Scouts, she stopped abruptly. Pointing to a nearby shelf, she exclaimed, "That loom! I cannot believe you have that loom! It's exactly the one I've been wanting, but haven't been able to find – anywhere. In fact, I just asked my husband to order the plans and make one for me. That loom was meant for me, and I'm so glad I came here today."

A customer needed a number of black hats for a humorous thirtieth birthday celebration. All the women guests were to wear black because they

A Miracle in Progress

were "in mourning" for the aging guest of honor. Joy Johnston told the woman that the shop rarely gets donations of black hats, but that she would check. That afternoon, she found at least twenty black hats in various bags of donations to the shop.

Customers have found items which stir childhood memories. Bren said, "I found a children's toy box horse, identical to the one that I sat on for my first birthday picture. Wow! What a treasure! Thank you!"

Another shopper, with tears in her eyes, clutched a small children's bench and said, "This is exactly like the bench I remember having as a child. I can't believe that I came here today, and this was waiting for me."

One day a customer brought a rather large, thick terry cloth towel to the counter. The cashier, noting the beautifully embroidered fire engine and the name *Rodney* on it, said, "This is a really lovely towel, and it looks brand new. Some child will love the fire engine on it, too." The customer smiled. "I know," she said. "It's amazing! I'm a fire Commissioner, and my grandson's name is Rodney. Can you believe it?"

Often shoppers are thrilled to find items that "feather their nests." Lil Swickard told the story of a delighted customer who found a nearly complete set of china that matched her wedding china. Another satisfied customer found a set of dishes identical to a set that she had recently purchased.

A Miracle in Progress

Before finding this treasure, she had constantly run short of dishes. Now she finally had enough. And as a bonus, she bought them at our half-price sale!

Shortly after a small electric organ was donated and put out on the sales floor, Greg Przybylinski came in and walked over to it. He spent some time examining it, then sat down and began to play. Soon customers and volunteers gathered around him to listen. Someone asked if he could play a favorite song, and he did. Then others began making requests and soon we had a songfest which lasted for almost an hour.

We learned that Greg, a disabled veteran, had been a professional musician, and obviously a very talented one. He came back and played for us several more times before he purchased the organ.

Greg Przybylinski's enjoyable organ entertainment brings in a donation from volunteer Dean Recktenwall.

A Miracle in Progress

Soon after, another larger organ was donated, and again Greg appeared. He helped to appraise it, and then entertained us. We are hoping that another organ is donated so that he will come back for a return engagement.

Duneland Resale is not only a place for finding sought-after items, but it is also a place for finding people. Kim Goldak tells us that twenty-some years ago, Susie Horan had been her husband Frank's friend and landlord while he was a college student in Chicago. When Frank and Kim began dating, Susie became Kim's friend, too. The friendship continued through their engagement and marriage, and after.

In time, the young couple moved away and, as often happens when time and distance separate people, they lost touch with Susie. One day while Kim was working as a cashier, she cried out in joy as Susie walked through the front door. It was touching to witness their reunion as they hugged and greeted each other. One can never predict what or even who will be found at Resale.

A Miracle in Progress

A Delightful Surprise

~ as told by a volunteer
  to Ann Howard, volunteer

A volunteer told this story about her family's friends from Holland, who frequently donate items and shop at Resale. They celebrate St. Nicholas Day in the traditional way by baking goodies for their friends and neighbors, leaving their gifts of candy and baked goods at the doors, then disappearing.

When shopping at Resale one day, our volunteer was delighted to discover a beautiful St. Nicholas mug made in Holland, and she knew that she had found the perfect gift for them. She would fill the mug with candy canes, bake her mother's famous ginger cookies and make hot chocolate. Then she would give them these treats for St. Nicholas Day.

As it happened, her friends were even more pleased than she had imagined. On the very day that the mother had donated numerous items, including her son's St. Nicholas mug, to Duneland Resale, our volunteer found the mug there and purchased it.

Later that day the son said, "Does anyone know what happened to my St. Nicholas mug? I can't find it anywhere."

A Miracle in Progress

The mother answered, "Oh, I am so sorry! I donated it to Duneland Resale. I thought you had outgrown it."

Of course, it was too late to reclaim the mug. It had already been sold and the son was very disappointed. What an amazing surprise they must have had on St. Nicholas Day when the beloved mug returned, full of delicious treats!

Coincidence or a small miracle? Readers, what do you think?

A Miracle in Progress

A Timely Blessing

~ *as told by a volunteer to Ann Howard, volunteer*

In the early days of Duneland Resale, when we volunteers were learning and finding our way through the ins and outs of running a resale shop, a woman came to the cash register with a handful of purchases. She had bought several of our lowest priced items, and the cashier knew from her appearance that life had been very difficult for her.

"My, what a lovely pair of pearl earrings," the cashier said, "And they look expensive." As she put them into the bag, she turned them over in her hand. "Well, look at this! These are pure gold, and these pearls look real, too."

The woman's eyes brightened, and much to the cashier's surprise, she picked up one of the earrings and bit into the pearl. "Oh, my goodness! You're right! No paint came off. I think they are definitely real!"

The cashier said, "Maybe you could get them appraised."

Hugging the bag to her chest, the woman started to cry. "Oh, I . . . I will. I'll do that . . . oh, thank you so much!"

The volunteer who shared this story says that even after all these years she can still picture the woman standing there, and realizes she had witnessed a miracle in the woman's life.

A Miracle in Progress

An Angel on My Shoulder

~ *by Brandon Fero, friend of Resale*

Brandon is the son of volunteer, Tammie Fero, and grandson of volunteers, Lil and Chuck Swickard.

In May of 2009, I was assigned as a driver to Third Platoon in Charlie Company, 2nd Battalion, 5th Cavalry Regiment, within the 1st Cavalry Division. We had been deployed in Iraq since late February and had endured fast-paced and difficult duty. Assigned to a Joint Security Station (JSS), our company of roughly 130 personnel acted autonomously within our assigned sector, branching out into the suburbs surrounding the Gold Wall, which partitions Sadr City proper from the main outskirts of Baghdad.

We of Charlie Company, a.k.a."Crazy Horse," were assigned to find terrorists – men of Sadr's private militia, al Qaeda, or any one of forty different political parties who were using kidnapping, extortion, blackmailing, or terrorism to impose their agenda onto the populace. In doing so, we also provided escorts for our financial teams to go to town hall meeting where our officers would sit down with community leaders and discuss what was needed to modernize and upgrade their living standards. It was one of those meeting days when I realized how greatly God

A Miracle in Progress

watched over me, and all of us, and just how deeply prayer can be felt.

As it was my third combat tour, I was assigned as a senior driver on an eight-and-a-half-ton MRAP truck and made the lead driver of my platoon. That day my Commanding Officer (CO) was finishing one of his meetings with the community leaders and was calling for an RTB (Return to Base.)

As we set out from the town hall, I was in a hurry to return for some rest and relaxation before we began our guard shifts the next morning. Because of extremely rough roads, I was driving 20 miles an hour, much slower than normal. My truck commander, Staff Sergeant Washington, a quiet, devout man with good experience and fair judgment, told me to slow down. I did so, but knowing how close we were to the base, I became anxious and soon started to speed up again. In a more forceful tone, he said, "Slow down now to 15 miles an hour!"

Approximately 600 feet from the entrance to base, it happened. The only thing I can remember was a deafening explosion that threw us around like rag dolls. In the chaos, my head whipped hard against my shoulder. Afterward, we all sat there, dumbfounded, as if in a fog. *What had happened?* Checking ourselves for injuries, it was hard to believe that there were none. We had been hit by an EFT, an Explosively Formed Projectile,

A Miracle in Progress

which is a tube packed with a high explosive that is set off by a trigger. The explosion propels a deadly copper "slug" that reaches a velocity of about 6,000 feet per second. We were thankful to be alive.

Next I realized there was no power. The truck was dead and we had no communications with the other trucks. SSG Washington used his portable radio to call and report that no one was injured and that we were going to begin clearing the area. Welty, realizing that his turret's battery was still operational, began scanning for the trigger man who had set off the device.

Washington and I shouted for the men to get out. Sgt. Stanley and Private Coffey, who was only 19 years old and the youngest of the platoon, barreled over towards the nearest houses to look in doors and sweep for the trigger man. Minutes later, we found him lying in a nearby pond, dead, caught in the explosion of his own device.

At one point during the attack, I looked up to find a rosary hanging from the CVRJ set that controls the jammer. It occurred to me that I had not felt that sixth sense of awareness that soldiers sometimes get when they are about to be hit. I had felt it before, in earlier tours, but not in this one. Before we left the town hall, I had been praying to Almighty God, and as we returned, I had been at peace, even calm. In my studies, I have learned that, at times of divine intervention, a person may

A Miracle in Progress

feel such a peace that he is not worried about himself.

Not until we had gotten back on the JSS and I had seen the other side of the truck did I see where the EFP had hit. It jarred me . . . the EFP slug had carved a ten-inch hole through the V12 diesel engine block, cut all the engine's and batteries' connections to the equipment and missed SSG Washington and me by a scant twelve inches.

I recalled that even though I had been in a hurry to get back, Sergeant Washington had insisted that I slow down. My speed at the time of the hit was 14 miles per hour. If I had been going just a bit faster, the slug would have hit both of us.

Christ and God were watching over all of us on that hot, dusty day in Baghdad, and I praise and thank Them for the opportunity to write about it now. I now know this – miracles do happen.

*　　*　　*

The prayers of family, churches, and of many good-hearted people across the nation for the men and women now deployed in war zones throughout the world are a powerful and defining force. I pray that God might bless those who read my story.

A Miracle in Progress

Life Is a Miracle!
Breathing! Seeing! Hearing!
Touching! Loving!

~ *by Dr. Dan Keilman, volunteer*

Duneland Resale is a miracle of teaming. Volunteers operate more than a million dollar business, and generous community members donate the goods which make that business possible. As faithful buyers regularly benefit from the volunteers who maintain the business, Resale enhances life for residents of four counties. With all this activity, love is spread among Resale volunteers, donors, and buyers.

Because of Resale donations, homes of those unable to pay utility bills are lit. Potentially homeless persons receive rent assistance so that they can maintain their own homes. Those in need of health services they cannot afford are able to pay for such services with assistance from Resale. Those needing love and companionship visit the aisles of the shop and find these treasures there, many times from Resale personnel.

With help from Resale, schools are able to afford educational services which had been beyond their purchasing power. One such school grant is used to train students in leadership skills which

A Miracle in Progress

they pass on to fellow students who need these skills to become better citizens and students.

Cancer survivors, who are supported by Resale, are grateful, and celebrate their blessings. A village in Africa has healthy water because our Director has gone there to work on the project. Hearts, minds, and souls are healed by counseling assistance provided by volunteer Resale personnel.

Churches teaming with Resale provide Christian principles which drive all behavior in the Resale community. Regardless of personal beliefs, everyone in this community, as a creature of God, is welcome, respected, and loved.

I, as a volunteer, live more fully because of the many miracles of Resale, and I have observed life-changing miracles in the lives of others. Here is one such miracle.

A lady who had given up on life because of many circumstances beyond her control, entrusted herself to Resale. She had no money and was living in her car. A generous donor provided her with gas money and a telephone card so that she could contact the world in search of some kind of work. She found a position which helped her move on in life and find friends and a place to live.

Soon, she began to concentrate on her skills and established a small business enterprise. She is a gifted lady, still in search of a position matching her talents and education. She professes that she is now a different person. I see signs of happiness

A Miracle in Progress

and confidence on her face and in her behavior. She is now able to bring help and love to others. Miracles beget miracles!

In another instance, a mother found her way into the shop. She had been given twenty-four hours to vacate the home in which she had been living. She had four children for whom she was responsible. Tomorrow they would be homeless. It was mid-winter and the weather was severe. They had no coats and very few clothes. Their needs were immediately addressed by Resale.

Thanks to a change of mind, the man who had driven her out of his home gave her a two-day extension. Given the extra time, she was able to get into a homeless shelter. Soon after, with her boss's help, she moved into a rented apartment, and was able to buy a car. A local church gave assistance to her and her children, and she found great support in a newly gained faith.

In time, she began to feel that she could again take control of her own life. Because she feared that the person who rejected her would find and punish her, she was determined to find resources to leave the local community and move away to be with her family, who would welcome her back. Within four months, with the help of many local people and agencies, she found these resources, and now lives near her family in another state. While she was here, she talked regularly about the miracles in her life. She said that the

A Miracle in Progress

new life she was living was a resurrection from the death of a life without belief in God and in herself.

Sometimes, the greatest miracles in life are the small ones. One afternoon as we were about to close the shop, someone brought in two love birds which they thought we could sell. What were we to do to with them? The day was almost over and the weekend was imminent.

Five minutes before closing time, two women walked into Resale. We asked them if they would like to buy the birds. Few looking for love birds come into the shop on a Friday afternoon! Resale personnel, however, are business-minded as well as community-minded, and soon the shoppers had heard at least fifty reasons to buy the birds.

It was a done deal. One of the shoppers, encouraged by her friend, bought the birds. Those lovebirds were assured of a new life! More important, two people were able to have an enriched life because of their compassion for two of God's simple creatures. Some of our greatest miracles are the surprising and uplifting creatures in our lives.

The greatest miracle in our lives is the love we have for one another. Resale is loving others. What we do for the least of our brothers and sisters is done for our Creator. When we love, we live in God, and God in us. Miracles are not accidents or coincidences. They are decisions backed by faith, hope, and love

A Miracle in Progress

A Bounty of Blessings

~ as told by a volunteer to Ann Howard. This volunteer, who wishes to remain anonymous, will be called Hope in this story.

Hope was at the cash register checking out a large purchase of linens, dishes and clothing. "You did well today," she said to the customer as she filled her bags.

"I really needed all this and it's such a blessing for me to find it," the woman said. She explained that she had escaped from a terrible domestic situation. "This is as far as my money took me. What I have here is everything I need. . . except for a bike for my son."

Touched by the woman's story, Hope suddenly realized that she knew of a man who fixed discarded bicycles and passed them on for only a small donation to sustain his work. Although she did not know how to reach him, she nevertheless offered to try to find a bicycle for the boy.

A short while later, on her way to take her son to his guitar lesson, she passed a yard full of bicycles and stopped to see the man in charge. To her surprise, he was the man she had been seeking.

"Oh, yes, I have plenty of bikes," he said. "What's the situation?" After she explained, he said, "Of course, I'd be glad to help this woman. It

A Miracle in Progress

would be best if she could come and choose the right bike for her son – and in this case, a donation won't be necessary." Hope was delighted. As she was leaving, the man, seeing the guitar on the car seat, asked who played it.

"My son," she said, and explained that she was on her way to take her son to his guitar lesson at Front Porch Music, which was nearby.

"Well, who's his teacher? He said. "My grandson Jeremiah used to teach there."

"You won't believe this," she said, laughing. "Jeremiah was my son's first guitar teacher."

The man told her that soon Jeremiah would be having a recital in Chicago as a requirement for his Master's Degree. Eagerly she and her family drove into Chicago to attend the concert and hear Jeremiah play. What a bounty of blessings this was for everyone!

A Miracle in Progress

How All the Pieces Fit Together

~ by Ann Howard, volunteer

One morning, during the height of the allergy season, I awakened with a pounding headache. My head felt as if it was overstuffed with cotton. All I wanted to do was snuggle back into my warm bed and sleep – just sleep. I groaned. *No such luck today.* It was my day to work at Duneland Resale, and I had *to* be there in an hour. "N-o-o-o," I groaned. *There was no way!*

Not only did I feel dreadful, but I was stressed, really stressed. I had been struggling to finish making a Peter Rabbit quilt before the birth of my grandchild, who seemed determined to arrive several weeks ahead of schedule. The clock was ticking. Easter was months past, and I had been searching in vain to find fabric printed with bunnies or carrots – something to add life to a rather ordinary looking quilt.

My last hope was to make a trip to a fabric superstore which was miles away, but I had not been able to squeeze any more into my overloaded schedule. *Should I call off work today? After all, I am a volunteer. No one is going to fire me for missing one day. Surely someone could fill in for me.* That settled it! *I would drag myself out of bed, beg off work, and go shopping!*

A Miracle in Progress

And then my conscience began to nag me. *What if no one's available to fill in on short notice?* There was always so much work to do, and often, not enough people to handle all of it. *Besides, the resale shop is doing so much for the community, and people really are depending on me. What should I do?*

The choices were playing tug-of-war in my aching head. Finally, my conscience won. I crawled out of bed, took two aspirins, dressed, and grumping all the way, trudged out the door. No doubt about it – I was Ann of Arc today!

The first thing I saw as I walked into the shop made me gasp in disbelief. Directly in front of me, just inside the door, sat a huge cardboard box filled with fabric pieces and quilt squares. I could not have missed it. On the very top were three large pieces of fabric – two with bunny prints and one with carrots.

These were exactly what I had been looking for – just what was needed to finish the quilt. And as a bonus, all three pieces blended perfectly with the colors in my quilt. I blinked to make certain that I wasn't hallucinating, but no – there they were.

When Joy heard my breathless account of this miraculous occurrence, she smiled. "That's God's way of thanking you for coming in to work today," she said. And I knew that she was right.

A Miracle in Progress

Life Saver

~ *as told by Jack Shoenfelder, volunteer,
to Ann Howard, volunteer*

Jack, our volunteer who teaches at a nearby college, at the end of every semester holds a drawing for the books in his bookcase. He tells his students that some books are old, some are new, some are valuable and some are not. Some could be resold for cash at the campus book store, but he really has no idea which. The luck is in the draw.

Recently he held the traditional drawing. After his last class, one of his students who had won a book, thanked him, then left.

Later in the week, she came to him and said, "I know you don't know it, but you saved my life this week, and I want to thank you."

He gave her a questioning look.

"I was financially in desperate shape. A collection agency was after me to pay an overdue forty dollar bill. I didn't know what I was going to do. When I won the book, I was able to sell it for forty-two dollars and pay that bill. I don't know how to thank you. I want to give you something, but I have nothing to give you . . . but this." She handed him a banana, then hugged him and walked away.

He cannot tell the story without tears in his eyes; we cannot listen to it without tears in ours.

In the Right Place

~ *by Kim Goldak, volunteer*

As I was at a local college registering for several classes, I chatted amiably with the student secretary for a little over 10 minutes. I was waiting for Tony, the head of the Student Union, who was coming to help me finish my application. It had been approximately 30 years since my school days, and I had a few concerns. Tony arrived and we began to discuss several different issues.

In the background I overheard the student secretary talking on the phone: "Can you tell me the results of my daughter's MRI?" she asked. She waited for a few moments, then said, "Abnormal? Abnormal . . . Please, could you tell me more than that? I've had some medical experience, and I can understand the terms. Please – tell me what the report says." Again, she waited. "What? Oh, no!"

I saw her worried expression turn to one of disbelief, then painful realization. She brushed away the tears that spilled down her cheeks.

"Tony, is she speaking about a problem in the brain?" I asked quietly. He nodded *yes*. I wrote my name and telephone number on a piece of paper, handed it to Tony and asked him to give it to the woman. I explained that I am a 10-year brain cancer survivor, and to some extent an

A Miracle in Progress

expert, as it is somewhat of a miracle that I am still alive and cancer-free. Although the recurrence rate is 100 percent, I have a strong feeling that I will be the exception to the rule.

Abruptly, the secretary left and hurried toward the restroom. It was then, somehow, that I knew I had to follow her. You see, I felt that I was there, in that spot, for just that reason. This timing was no coincidence – it was my job to reassure her and offer to help in any way I could.

I walked into the restroom and approached the woman very carefully. "I know you don't know me, but I couldn't help overhearing your conversation just now. I'm a 10-year brain cancer survivor and I want you to know that I would be so willing to help you in any way possible."

* * *

Yes, now I know why I am and will be the exception to the rule. I am meant to give hope and help to all who need it.

A Miracle in Progress

Slated for Success

~ by Ann Howard, volunteer

In September I was decorations chairman for my women's church guild's Back-to-School luncheon. My husband Frank, a woodworker, cut out several small wooden slates for me. I painted them black, then wrote "Welcome" on them with white chalk.

The following spring the guild president asked me if I could make more slates for the annual fundraiser, which that year was to be a luncheon for retired school teachers. I asked my husband whether he could make more slates. Overwhelmed with projects of his own, he said that he would do so, but he would get to them when he had more time.

As the deadline approached with no sign of any slates, I was uneasy. My calendar, too, was quickly filling with activities and, even if Frank finished them in time, I was not certain that I would have time to paint them. I considered shopping around for ready-made slates, just in case, but I had no clue where to find them.

One morning several days later, less than a week before the luncheon, I went to work at Resale. As I took my post at the cash register, I was surprised to see a small school slate which a customer had placed on the counter with her other purchases. I said to a fellow volunteer, "That slate

A Miracle in Progress

is exactly what I'm looking for, but I need five of them. I wonder where I could find them."

"Well, look right over there," she said, gesturing toward a nearby table. "There are about five more of them."

I turned, and indeed, there they were – five more slates, the very size that I needed. There was no question about it – this small miracle was a large blessing for me, and for my husband, too.

A Miracle in Progress

Miracles and More Miracles

*~ as told by Mary Louise Reey, volunteer,
to Ann Howard, volunteer*

"Miracles? Miracles! Have I seen miracles?" Mary Louise said, as she gave me a "you-must-be-kidding" look. "Oh, my, have I seen miracles! Just listen to this!" And then she began to tell her stories of the miracles she has witnessed at Duneland Resale

Mary Louise, a devoted and seemingly tireless volunteer, works almost every day. When she began working with the jewelry, she immediately realized the need for a jeweler's loupe (small magnifying glass) to properly examine and evaluate the donations. Much to her surprise, in no time one was donated.

Certainly this experience alone could be chalked up as a fortunate coincidence. But wait – there is much more to tell. Soon, with jewelry overflowing all available containers, she decided that she needed a cabinet in which to store the excess. If you have not already guessed, almost immediately one was donated.

As more such incidents occurred, she began to see a pattern – one of her prayers answered and, indeed, one of miracles at work. Her experiences continued to reinforce her belief.

A Miracle in Progress

One day she dropped her only iron and demolished it. What a bother! Now she would have to buy a new one. Believe it or not, before she had the chance to shop for one, an iron, the same brand as hers but a better model, appeared. And as always, the price at Duneland Resale was just right.

Wanting to prepare a special treat for Dan Johnston's birthday celebration, Mary Louise dug out a favorite recipe. Although this project was a great idea, she discovered that she had given away her two rolling pins. Obviously, she would have to borrow or buy one.

Again, she was awed by what happened next. A few days later she was delighted to see that a brand new pink rolling pin had been donated, and she purchased it immediately.

Of course, Dan and those volunteers who enjoyed her delicious dessert felt that they were the real benefactors of this miracle!

Mary Louise's final story is rich with miracles. She was overcome with joy when her twin granddaughters were born, and she decided that the perfect baby gift would be a pair of rocking chairs. Her lovely antique rocker would be ideal for rocking those babies and, oh, how she wished that she had two of them! But she knew that finding an identical rocker was next to impossible.

A Miracle in Progress

Although she thought of other gift possibilities, she could not get the idea of two matching rocking chairs out of her mind. Within a short period of time, the most astounding thing happened. A rocker, identical to hers, except in color, was donated – another answered prayer.

Knowing that her son and daughter-in-law, who lived far away, needed the chairs as soon as possible, she decided that shipping Fed-Ex was her best option. When she called the Fed-Ex office to see if they had boxes large enough for the rockers, the clerk assured her that the boxes were available; however, upon arriving there with the chairs, she was disappointed to learn that there were none large enough. *Now what?* she thought.

At this point, many people would have been discouraged, but not Mary Louise. She was on a mission and she was not to be deterred! Her next stop was a nearby furniture store, where she inquired about buying large boxes. The manager not only found a box large enough for both rockers, but also he gave it to her at no charge.

Buoyed up by his generosity, she returned to the Fed-Ex office. But oh, how she dreaded to hear the cost of shipping those two chairs!

The flustered clerk apologized, saying that the computers were down and she was not at all sure what to charge for the shipment. After stewing over the problem for a few minutes, she said, "Oh, let's just make it $15.00. Is that okay?"

A Miracle in Progress

Mary Louise was speechless, but quickly nodded *yes*. How grateful she was for the miraculous blessings she had received that day!

Soon Grandma's lovely gifts arrived, and Grandma herself flew out to meet her two tiny angels. She and her daughter-in-law painted both rockers the same mellow, antique color, and the rockers have been used to rock the twins ever since.

Not only rocking chairs, but a variety of other fine furniture is donated to Resale.

A Miracle in Progress

A Treasure Found

~ by Wendy Marciniak, friend of Resale

I had only one more trip down the basement stairs before I would finally have all of the Christmas decorations put away. The only things left were my little crystal Avon church, some glass candlesticks, and a small crystal angel given to me by my mother-in-law. These things, along with the manger scene, were always the first things I put up, and the last to come down.

I had forgotten to bring up the boxes for these last few items on my previous trip to the basement. So by carefully placing everything in both arms, I started down the stairs.

I don't know exactly what shifted in which arm, but the next thing I knew, my little glass church tumbled down the stairs and broke into a million pieces when it hit the concrete floor. I was heartsick. That little church reminded me so much of my own church, with its old-fashioned design and steeple, and even a stained glass window. It sat on a little base that lit up, and when it was turned on, it just glowed.

Of course, I contacted Avon to see if it could be replaced. I was told *No*, that item had been

A Miracle in Progress

discontinued a few years back. After that, for months I searched e-bay, the Salvation Army, Goodwill stores, and of course, Duneland Resale. No luck! Every time I went to any of those places, I looked, even though by then most Christmas items had been put away.

Summer came and went. I had pretty much forgotten about the church. Then the week before Thanksgiving, I went to the Resale shop to drop off a few donations.

Back then, the shop had just moved to its second location, the old Zip Foods store on the corner of Calumet and Wabash. After handing over my bags, I noticed the shelves of holiday items. Of course, I was drawn to them, just out of habit.

Don't you know, sitting on a shelf, just waiting for me was a little crystal Avon church in perfect condition?

I know I squealed, because Lil Swickard came over to me, and before she could say, "Are you okay?" I told her the story of how I had broken my little church and had been looking for one ever since. She was very happy for me, but didn't seem surprised, since people find long lost treasures there all the time.

I don't know why anyone would give up this precious little church, but I am so glad they did. You can bet that I have carried it carefully down the stairs all by itself, safely in its box, ever since!

A Miracle in Progress

A Christmas Blessing

~ as told by Aleta Ailes, volunteer,
  to Ann Howard, volunteer

It was nearly Christmas and shopping time was quickly running out. A look of urgency was visible on the shoppers' faces as they scurried about Duneland Resale to find that last gift or two before the shop closed.

Yes, it was Christmas, a time when children should be happy. And Aleta wanted so much to make a child happy. Because she had chosen a wish list from the Salvation Army children's Angel tree at the front, she knew that this child wanted a Monopoly game.

She was determined to give him what he wanted, and she hoped it wasn't too late to find one. She wanted to find the game at a reasonable price, and she knew that Duneland Resale would be the best place to look.

As Aleta walked through the shop, she shook her head. The disarray and the partially empty shelves were proof of what an unbelievably busy day it had been. Her heart sank as she approached the toy shelves, which were practically bare. All she could think was, "Please, please let there be one."

She stopped, and a grin spread across her face as she saw the only game that was left – a

A Miracle in Progress

Monopoly game. She was very excited as she told this story of her Christmas miracle. Then, beaming, she pointed upward and said, "Prayers go up, and blessings come down."

God loves a cheerful giver.
And God is able to provide you with every blessing in abundance, so that you may always have enough of everything and may provide in abundance for every good work.
II Corinthians 9:7, 8 (RSV)

A Miracle in Progress

Ask and Ye Shall Receive

*~ as told by Dan Johnston, volunteer,
to Ann Howard, volunteer*

Our Resale friend Lorrie Woycik called to ask if, by chance, there was a sofa-bed at the shop. She said, "A family needs one because they have no bed."

"There isn't one right now," Dan Johnston said, "but let's give it a little time and we'll see what we can do." That day was busy, as was the next morning, which flew by as he ran errands. His cell phone rang as he entered the shop.

"Dan, have you found a sofa-bed yet?" Lorrie asked.

Looking around, he said, "Well, it looks like a couch came in while I was gone. Let me go check it out, and I'll call you back." By now, you may have guessed that the couch was a sofa-bed in excellent condition, which Dan immediately gave to the family.

A few days later, Lorrie called again and said, "The people who have the couch have called and thanked me at least 18 times because they are so grateful to have a place to sleep. Thank you for what you did for them."

Of course, we know that this was not a case of what we did for them, but what God did. Such miraculous occurrences are not unusual at Resale.

A Miracle in Progress

We no longer accept large appliances, but there was a time when we did. For example, someone who needed a refrigerator, but could not afford one, would call to see if we had one. Dan would assure the caller that he would see if one was available. We could count on one of two scenarios: He would find that one had already been donated, or one would come in soon after the request. When these miracles happen, we say, "Thank you, Lord. You did it again!"

The Miracle of Love

~ by Dr. Dan Keilman, volunteer

Many celebrations in our culture focus primarily on drinking and personal revelry. Often weddings are the exceptions to this rule. While the celebration of a great number of weddings includes alcoholic beverages, the focus is on positive reactions to the love shown in the wedding ceremony, as well as the social interaction among those attending it.

My son Steven's recent wedding met the latter description. Those who attended recognized the singular love involved in the relationship of the marrying couple and the union of two families brought together by the marriage.

As a father, I was excited and filled with positive thoughts as we entered the church for the ceremony. Preparation for it had gone well, and one sensed a singular joy in those attending the ceremony. I expected love miracles from this marriage, and I witnessed one early in the marriage ceremony.

The priest included a brief homily after the exchange of vows. He told this story. Prior to the ceremony, he had had private sessions with the couple. As part of these sessions, he asked each one, separate from the other, why each wanted to get married. My son's response was, "I want to get

A Miracle in Progress

married so that I can be a couple with Marie and make a difference for other people." My son wanted to develop a love relationship with his bride which would lead to developing greater love relationships with others.

Every child is a miracle; a true marriage is likewise. And, if the marriage leads to compliance with the invitation to love one's neighbor as oneself, the miracles continue.

A Miracle in Progress

The Message

~ *by Ann Howard, volunteer*

One Sunday after church I had an amazing experience. As my friend Leigh Pell and I walked outside together, we were shocked to see these words scrawled in chalk on the blacktop parking lot: "I WOULD LIKE TO MURDER THE WORLD. I HATE RELIGION!"

Lee's husband, Tim, who had followed us outside, went back inside to get a bucket of water to wash away the hateful message, but it haunted me as I drove away. The experience had been unsettling, and I wondered who would be angry and unhappy enough to write such things.

Deciding that a cup of my favorite coffee might help boost my spirits, I drove toward the restaurant, which was on the other side of the railroad tracks. Just as I approached the tracks, however, the gates came down for an oncoming train. *Great! Just great! First, that awful writing and now I have to sit here and wait for a train! What else could go wrong today?* There I sat, fuming.

Watching the train inching its way along the track did nothing to lighten my mood. Now I would have an even longer wait. And then I saw it. On one of the cars there was graffiti and also writing – large, neatly printed letters spanning the

A Miracle in Progress

entire side. I read the message: HOW CAN I BE MAD WHEN THERE IS SO MUCH BEAUTY IN LIFE? I was stunned! *Who could have written it – and, why?* I grabbed my pen and scribbled the words on my church bulletin so that I would not forget them.

As I sat there, those inspiring words totally obliterated the impression of the angry ones on the parking lot. I felt uplifted.

Somehow, I knew right then that the words on the train car were meant just for me. I had been in a hurry – impatient and irritable – but God's timing slowed me down and allowed me to read that important message. God's small miracle transformed my mood that day, and the memory of it comes back to me when I am tempted to let negative thoughts weigh me down.

A *Miracle in Progress*

Special Delivery

~ *by Ann Howard, volunteer*

At a monthly board meeting, our Director Dan Johnston began going through the list of proposed monetary donations when he came to a sizeable donation to be shared by all the area homeless shelters.

He paused for a moment, looked at the group and, for a reason even unknown to him at the time, he said, "Wait a second, just . . . wait a second. I don't know why, but Gabriel's Horn Shelter just popped into my mind and I really think that, instead of donating to all the shelters right now, I would like the entire donation to go to Gabriel's Horn."

His wife Joy gave him a puzzled look, then nodded *yes,* and the rest of the Board approved his request. An hour later, after the shop had opened, Dan asked Mary Louise and me to watch for a homeless woman who was about to arrive. The Township Trustee had called to find her a ride to Gabriel's Horn, the only shelter with a vacancy that day.

For several days, this woman had wandered about without shelter, adequate clothing or food. It was a brutally cold windy April with temperatures in the low 30's and below, and there had been light snow all week. After sleeping for two nights in the

A Miracle in Progress

park in the freezing weather, Jennifer,* pale and shivering, had wandered into the Trustee's office and asked for help. The Trustee called Dan, who, of course, immediately volunteered to give her warm clothing and other necessities and then drive her to the shelter.

When the frail woman-child walked through our door, Mary Louise and I blinked back tears at the sight of her. This fragile waif wore a skimpy warm-up jacket, a tee shirt, tattered jeans and frayed cotton tennis shoes. Teeth chattering, she spoke softly, "I... I am so cold."

Speechless, we simply opened our arms to her. Immediately, she came to us. Each of us gave her a gentle hug and she hugged us back.

When we asked if she would like to choose a suitcase and some warm clothing, she smiled and said, "Oh, yes! Thank you!" After choosing a large suitcase, we took her to the coat rack, where she pulled off a warm jacket and put it on. "I love this one," she said, and never took it off.

Eagerly, she found several sweaters, including one with the initial J on it, which she said must have been meant for her. She chose shirts, pants, other necessary items and finally, only one lightweight pair of shoes. At that point we could find no sturdy shoes in her size.

Joy, smiling, approached us and took the girl's hand. "Hello, Jennifer," she said, "I'm very glad you're here and I hope you've found the

A Miracle in Progress

things you need." Joy continued, "You know, it's almost lunch time and I'm really hungry. Why don't you join me for a nice, hot lunch." Without hesitation, Jennifer followed her into the kitchen.

As she began to relax, the girl told Joy her heartbreaking story. She had fallen in love with the wrong person, a young man her mother intensely disliked. Soon after, in a fit of rage, her mother had kicked her out of the house.

The immature, inexperienced young couple quickly married and, unable to support themselves, soon ran out of money and hope. They argued constantly. The young husband, frustrated and angry, was unable to sustain himself, let alone a wife, and soon he kicked Jennifer out of their apartment.

Having nowhere to go and no one to help her, she wandered about in the cold for several days until she found the Township Trustee's office. From there she came to Resale.

Joy asked Jennifer how she had survived outdoors during the freezing weather and the girl told her incredible story. She had walked and walked all around our town until nighttime. By then she was tired, hungry and afraid – everything seemed worse in the dark. Hoping for some shelter and wanting to become invisible, she walked into the park.

For a time she sat, and then exhausted, she gave up and lay down, curling up into a ball on the

A Miracle in Progress

ground. Cold, miserable, she lay awake for a while, but eventually fell into a fitful sleep.

Suddenly startled and half awake, she sat up. She shivered. Someone or something was there with her, watching her. As her eyes adjusted to the dark, she saw a large brown Labrador Retriever staring directly at her.

Warily, they watched each other for a time, until she timidly called to the dog. He stood perfectly still at first, but eventually he began to inch toward her, step by step. At last she coaxed him to her and, mustering her courage, reached out to pet him. Never letting his gaze leave her, he allowed her to pet him until finally he relaxed and curled up next to her. Eventually she put her arms gently around him and they lay together, keeping each other warm and safe until they both fell asleep.

The dog stayed with her for two nights. It seemed to us that God must have sent that dog to Jennifer to keep her from freezing.

We could hardly bear to think of a young person in such desperate straits, and we were so grateful to be able to help her, even temporarily. Our hope was that the caregivers at the shelter could put her on track for her future safety and well-being.

Wearing a lovely smile and warm clothing, Jennifer thanked all of us as she left with Dan. He carried her suitcase full of clothes and necessities,

A Miracle in Progress

by then including two pairs of shoes, one of which will be the subject of a related story entitled "If the Shoe Fits." (Stay tuned . . .)

When Jennifer and Dan arrived at Gabriel's Horn, the director welcomed them both. Then she said, "Oh, Dan, I am so glad to see you! I planned to call you today to see if Duneland Resale could possibly spare any funds for us. We desperately need your help."

Remembering his sudden inspiration that morning – his epiphany – Dan was speechless. After a moment, he managed to say, "Well . . . just this morning we voted to make a rather large donation to this shelter." She was tearful, unable to speak for a moment – as was Dan.

Later, when Dan told us about the director's request, we asked how he could have known that Resale should donate to that particular shelter, on that particular day. He was thoughtful for a few moments, and then he smiled. Looking upward, he pointed to the sky. "I guess it was airmail, Special Delivery," he said. There was not a dry eye among us!

For obvious reasons, the name of the young girl was changed. And, in case you are wondering what happened to the dog. . . Joy did go back to the park several times to find this canine Earth Angel. Much to her regret, she never did.

FIVE
A Good Laugh

As well as sharing the stories of miracles we have witnessed, we also want to relate a few of our experiences that made us laugh.

If the Shoe Fits . . .

~ as told by Joy and Dan Johnston, volunteers,
  to Ann Howard

Joy and Dan Johnston are two extremely kind, compassionate and generous people. In addition to directing the Resale mission, they devote much time to helping others. They shared this story.

When they were visiting an area homeless shelter, Joy, who is a nurse, was concerned about a diabetic man wearing worn-out shoes that were much too small for him.

She mulled over the problem for a while, then said, "Dan, could you step outside for a minute?"

Dan looked at her. "Okay, but why?"

She raised an eyebrow and gave him a determined look. "Just . . . come with me."

He shrugged his shoulders and followed her into the hall.

A Miracle in Progress

Once they were alone, she said, "That man has diabetes. Look at his shoes. They're worn out. Worse than that, they're much too small, and they're obviously constricting his feet. He must be getting blisters, and that could be very dangerous for him."

He said, "Well, okay . . . okay, but what do you suggest we do about it?"

"Dan, I really think your shoes will fit him. We're going to give him your shoes."

"What?" he said, "Come on, Joy, these are my new Rockports. I just got them broken in and they are very comfortable."

"Exactly! He needs them more than you do. Just. . . give. . . me. . .your. . .shoes."

He knew that she was right and he also knew there was no point in arguing with her. The matter was not negotiable. Dan, being Dan, nodded *yes*, and reluctantly gave the man his shoes.

Of course, as luck would have it, they fit perfectly. Smiling, the man thanked Dan.

"Well, what do you want me to do now?" Dan said.

"Just go back and put his shoes on."

"Listen," he said, "if they don't fit him, they won't fit me."

"Really, you can't drive without shoes, and I can't drive the truck. Besides, it's freezing outside. Just go ahead . . . and put them on," Joy said, smirking. Again, the eyebrow. . .

A Miracle in Progress

"Okay, okay. . ." He sighed, then retrieved the shoes and put them on. (Just for the record, he swears that his feet ached all the way home.)

Several weeks later, the man came to the shop to thank Joy for her kindness and Dan for his shoes.

We have laughed repeatedly at this story; furthermore, we now know that Dan would not only give someone the shirt off his back, but also the shoes from his feet!

Whatever Goes Around. . .

Now, rewind to the story of Jennifer, the homeless girl who was getting Resale assistance – food, clothing, and necessities. At one point Mary Louise and I had found everything she needed, except for a warm, sturdy pair of shoes. We had looked through all the shoes with no luck, when Joy came to help.

After her fruitless search for a suitable pair, she was thoughtful for a moment, and then looked down at her own shoes. They were sturdy and warm – and also brand new.

"Well. . . why don't you try mine on?" she said.

Jennifer put them on. "Oh, these are perfect! They feel so good. Thank you! Thank you!"

A Miracle in Progress

After the girl walked away, Joy rolled her eyes, smiled and whispered, "Wouldn't you know it?"

Just then we three had the same thought – of Joy's insisting that Dan give away his shoes at the homeless shelter. We all started laughing. Of course, Dan, more than anyone, enjoyed the story and thoroughly appreciated the irony of it.

Many are grateful for Resale's fine selection of shoes. Joan Jasen, former shoe chairman, and her daughter restock the shoe shelves.

A Miracle in Progress

One Man's Trash...

~ by Ann Howard, volunteer

June, one of our customers, told the story of her father who, much to his family's frustration, saves everything. She and her mother had been on a mission to persuade him to get rid of some of his "treasures" which clutter their home. Finally, he did part, reluctantly, with a few items, which were then donated to Duneland Resale.

One day, while June was browsing in the shop, she discovered the perfect gift for him – a battery-powered television and stereo combination which was very reasonably priced. After all, he had been such a good sport about parting with his beloved things, and she wanted to reward him. Without hesitation, she purchased her "find" and rushed to her parents' home to give it to her dad.

She was disappointed when her mother said that he had gone fishing. "But stay a while. He should be home soon," her mother said. June showed her mother the gift she had bought, and her mother said, "You know, he used to have something like that. I'm sure he'll like it."

When her dad came home, June met him outside and dragged him into the house. "Look, Dad, I have a surprise for you. I bought it today at Duneland Resale."

A Miracle in Progress

"Well, well," he said, "let's see it." He walked over to the television/stereo, looked it over, and said, "You know, I used to have something like that."

In case you haven't guessed, he was right. June, in her effort to do something nice for her father, had bought back his old television/stereo combination – the one that she had donated earlier to Duneland Resale.

"So why'd you give it away if you knew I liked it so much?" he teased, and they all shared a good laugh.

A Miracle in Progress

Tug o' War

~ as told by Dan Johnston, volunteer,
  to Ann Howard

Our shop faces the same challenges as any other business. Shoplifters and, in particular, habitual shoplifters, continue to be a problem. We were aware that one of our frequent shoppers was a shop-lifter; however, we could never "catch her in the act." We knew that eventually the opportunity would come, and we were waiting for the right moment to confront her and end the scam. It was simply a matter of time.

Then one day, into the shop she came in her oversized full-length coat, undoubtedly lined with large pockets to conceal her loot. A volunteer, who was inconspicuously observing her, saw her handling an elegant blue dress which, after a few minutes, mysteriously disappeared. It was not on the rack nor in her hands. Where, oh where else could it be, except in "the coat"?

As he nonchalantly followed her to the cash register, he noted with satisfaction that a part of the missing blue dress was trailing from underneath the hem of her coat. Fortunately, she was the only customer at the counter.

As she checked out, he said in a voice that only the cashier and the woman could hear, "Add ten dollars to her bill for the blue dress."

A Miracle in Progress

The cashier looked puzzled and the customer spun around and snarled at him, "What blue dress? I don't have any blue dress!"

He said quietly, "The one hidden inside your coat."

She spewed out a torrent of angry words, grabbed her package, and rushed toward the door.

The man, ordinarily a soft-spoken and patient gentleman, said that right then, something inside him snapped. *That's it! Enough is enough!*

He ran out the door behind her. As he reached her, he grabbed the exposed piece of the dress and pulled it until most of the dress was out of the coat and trailing on the ground. Glaring at him, she snatched up the other end of the dress, and a major Tug-o'-War ensued. It was a good match which, eventually he won. As he claimed his prize, she cursed him and stomped off to her car.

It is no surprise that she has never returned. We have laughed many times at the thought of this mild-mannered man who turned into a super-hero to reclaim our stolen merchandise. In retrospect, we realized that there were actually two winners that day. We wondered if the woman also recognized her good fortune. Losing a game of Tug-o'-War and the blue dress was far better than being turned over to the local police.

A Miracle in Progress

Lifeline Tales

~ *as told by Nancy Ruffing, volunteer,*
  to Ann Howard, volunteer

One of the ways Duneland Resale shows its appreciation to its senior volunteers is to provide Lifeline service for those who are over 70 years old. Lifeline is a small device worn around the neck which signals for help in the case of an emergency.

This support has been received with enthusiasm and gratitude by our volunteers. Unfortunately, both Laurie Ream and Dorothy Zenci have had falls and were unable to get up by themselves. In each case, they used their Lifelines to call for help.

Another "satisfied customer," Nancy, who has a slight hearing loss, appreciates the fact that the Lifeline blinks when the telephone rings. One day, when a service man was working on her television, she learned about Lifeline's prompt and clear response.

When he accidentally bumped the Lifeline box, which sits beside the television set, a very loud voice immediately boomed forth: "NANCY, ARE YOU ALL RIGHT? DO YOU NEED HELP?" Startled, both she and the service man started to laugh.

A Miracle in Progress

Then Nancy recalled a story told to her by the man who had originally set up her Lifeline. One of his customers is a gentleman who greatly appreciates the security and other benefits of his Lifeline, with one exception. Every time he hugs someone, he sets it off, booming voice and all. We can only hope that this inconvenience does not stifle his warmth and affection. Definitely, he has a dilemma: To hug, or not to hug – that is the question!

A Miracle in Progress

Trapped!

~ *by Ann Howard, volunteer*

Nicole, who was pregnant with her son Jaxon, and her mother-in-law Chrystal were shopping at Duneland Resale. After trying on several maternity outfits, Nicole, most anxious to go and find more bargains in the shop, hurriedly dressed.

When she tried the door knob, to her surprise, it would not turn. *Okay, if you don't succeed at first. . .* she reasoned, then tried again, and again. The door would not budge. *Fine! I'll have to push the silly door open.* No luck that time, either. She took a deep breath and pushed even harder, but the door was immobile. *Well, this is crazy – just crazy! Now, what?* she thought.

"Chrystal?" she said. There was no answer. "Chrystal?" she said a bit louder.

"What, Coley? I'm right over here. Oh, you should see this darling jacket!"

"Uh, I'd like to, but first, could you come and help me open this door? I'm stuck in here."

"What? Coley, you're kidding! You're stuck?" Chrystal chuckled. "Well, keep calm. I'll see if I can help. Okay, here goes." She tried the door several times, then said, "Well, you're right. You certainly are stuck in there!" By now, both women were laughing.

A Miracle in Progress

Nicole looked around her. Who would believe that she had gotten trapped in this tiny cubicle? Well, things could be worse. At least she didn't have claustrophobia.

"Coley, I have an idea. I'm going to lie down on the floor and look up under the door to see if I can figure this out." Nicole heard shuffling noises and a groan or two, then looked down to see her mother-in-law's hand and the side of her face.

"Well, I'll be . . . there's just no wiggle room here. I can see your feet, Coley, but that's about all." She sighed. Now, if I can just get untangled and get up from here. . ."

Nicole heard tell-tale noises and she could vividly picture her mother-in-law's contortions. "I bet you're putting on a good show out there, Chrystal." With that, both women dissolved in giggles.

Somewhat recovered, Chrystal managed to say, "Yes, I could probably sell tickets for this performance. Okay, now. . . I'm upright again, and I'm going to go and get you some help."

"That's the best idea yet!"

In a few minutes, Nicole heard Dan Johnston introducing himself to Chrystal and asking what the trouble was. Chrystal's explanation of Nicole's predicament was punctuated by Dan's and her laughter.

A Miracle in Progress

"Let me try the door," he said. After some rattles, taps, and thumps, he said, "You're right. It's really stuck." Then to Nicole, "Are you going to be okay in there for a few more minutes?" Assured that she was, he said, "Okay, I'll get some tools, and I'll be right back."

True to his word, he returned shortly. Nicole looked down as he slid a screwdriver under the door and said, "I think the best way to do this is to remove the doorknob. If you'll loosen the screws inside, I'll work on the ones out here."

Luckily, he and Nicole were an efficient team, and Dan did not have to call on the Jaws of Life to free her. In no time the job was done, and the prisoner was set free. Besides, there was more good news. The women not only had plenty of shopping time left, but also they had a great story to tell.

A Miracle in Progress

Wind Power

~ *as told by Dan Johnston, volunteer,*
  to Ann Howard, volunteer

Dan told this story about his good friends, a married couple who are responsible for his involvement in the Zambia water project. Michael is an easy-going man, who talks almost as slowly as he moves. Peggy, just the opposite, is energetic and enthusiastic, always busy with one project or another.

One day, bursting with ideas, Peggy was reciting a lengthy laundry list of things that absolutely needed to be done. Michael, taking all this in, waited for her to finish. Then giving her a steady look, he said, "Well, now, Peggy, just who do you think is going to do all of this?"

She beamed. "Why Michael, you are, of course!" she said.

Both Dan and Michael laughed, because they knew she was exactly right.

It is rumored that Dan, with a mischievous gleam in his eye, has said that he can very closely identify with Michael's situation. It seems that he, too, is often swept along by a most gusty wind to take on many unexpected projects. This rumor, however, remains unsubstantiated.

A Miracle in Progress

The Episode of the Traveling Pants

~ *by Ann Howard, volunteer*

One day hysterical laughter from the dressing room area drew a crowd of curious volunteers and shoppers who were curious to see what the commotion was all about. It seems that after Anna had gone into the dressing room to try on a pair of leather pants, she had remained there for an unusually long time. At her request, however, we can only say that she was in there for an "unspecified" amount of time; the exact length of her stay will remain classified to protect her dignity.

After her friend had asked several times if everything was okay in there, if there was a problem, Anna, giggling, finally admitted that she could not get out of those clingy, skin-tight pants. Soon she and her friend were overcome with laughter, and undoubtedly her weakened state must have only complicated her attempts to wiggle free.

Even Houdini might have found this predicament challenging. Furthermore, during her contortions to extricate herself from those pants which now must have seemed permanently bonded to her body, her socks somehow got caught up in her pant legs, gumming up the works even more.

A Miracle in Progress

Where, oh where, is a video camera at times like this? The bystanders could only imagine her gyrations as this slapstick comedy played out within the confines of that tiny dressing room.

When she finally escaped, unharmed, from the two-legged prison and the bystanders' laughter subsided, someone asked why she had wanted to get the leather pants in the first place. She said that she wanted to wear them while riding her Huffy bike, to impress her children.

Unfortunately, there is no information as to whether, in the end, she risked all and purchased the leather pants. One could only imagine her again squeezing into them, riding off on her Huffy bike and impressing her children.

There was, however, speculation that her children would be even more impressed at the effort she would have to make to escape those pants! If she realized her dream to the full extent, we could call this story "The Episode of the Traveling Pants."

A Miracle in Progress

The Tale of the Irresistible Blouse

~ *as told by Joy Johnston, volunteer,
to Ann Howard, volunteer*

As Joyce Recktenwall walked through Resale after working her shift, a flash of yellow caught her eye. The sunny colored madras blouse practically jumped out at her and called, "Buy me! Buy me!"

She was immediately transported to her college days when she worked in the kitchen of the Student Union. Earning a dollar and a quarter an hour, she splurged on very few things, but she fell in love with a madras blouse she had seen in a shop window. She simply had to have it and saved her money until she could finally buy it. Joyce was very excited because it was the first purchase she had ever made on her own.

And here was another madras blouse. It was perfect for her! She checked the label. *Great – it was J.Crew!* The price tag said three dollars. She smiled. *How could anyone resist such a bargain? How could she resist?* And so she bought it.

Not only did Joyce wear it to meetings and lunches out, but also for everyday outings. For a time it seemed that she and the blouse were nearly inseparable. Finally she decided she had worn it so much that people would think she owned only one blouse, and so she donated it back to Resale. (Only

A Miracle in Progress

women would understand this line of reasoning! Men will scratch their heads over her decision.)

Sorting clothing in the back room of the shop, Joy Johnston saw the flash of color and noticed that Joyce, looking hesitant, was holding up a madras blouse.

"I'm thinking of donating it," Joyce said, "but I can't make up my mind."

The cheerfully colored blouse seemed to wave its sleeves at Joy and shout, "Hey, look at me! Aren't I pretty?" *Yes, indeed, the blouse was pretty, and she loved the green, yellow and cranberry colors.* The madras blouse brought back such fun memories of hootenannies and fun times in the sixties. *That blouse was meant for her! And at Resale prices, how could she go wrong?*

"Well, be sure you want to part with it, because if you donate it, I'm buying it!" Joy said.

Joyce thought for a few minutes, then said, "I've worn it so often for several years now, and I'm really trying to make my wardrobe more neutral. Yes, I'm definitely donating it. Go for it!"

And so Joy bought it. She wore the blouse everywhere. It was just right for many occasions and she felt good each time she wore it. Eventually, though, she had worn it so much that she was ready for a change. Besides, she had plenty of other clothes in her closet. If she donated it back to Resale, then someone might enjoy it as much as she had. And so, back it went.

A Miracle in Progress

A week or so later, Joy was working on the sales floor when she saw the blouse worn by a customer whose back was turned. It had to be the same blouse and it seemed to call out to her, "Here I am! See? I've still got it! Someone loves me!" It looked so pretty that Joy had a moment of regret about parting with it so easily. Then the customer turned around and Joy started to chuckle. It was her friend Pam Wheelock.

"Pam, I love your blouse. You have great taste but. . . I have to ask you – by chance, did you buy it here?"

"Why, yes, as a matter of fact I did," Pam said. "I couldn't resist it, and it's become a staple of my wardrobe. I've worn it to dinner, working, shopping – everywhere – and people keep giving me compliments on it."

"Well, it looks great on you," Joy said, thinking that it actually looked better on Pam than it had on her. When Joy told Pam the story of the blouse – or at least as much as she knew – the two friends shared a hearty laugh.

Pam said, "Wouldn't it be great if the blouse were like a book in the library? Then we could look up its history to see who had owned it out before us. Maybe we should sew a piece of fabric in the neck and pass along a marking pen with the blouse so that each owner along the way could sign it."

A Miracle in Progress

No doubt this irresistible blouse has stories to tell, and perhaps one or more of you who is reading this book is privileged to be part of its colorful past.

Joy said that it is appropriate that Pam is one of the several owners of this blouse because she is such a strong advocate of recycling. In fact, Pam owns a pet toy and pet supply business, Purrfectplay. All her merchandise is made from organic and recycled materials, which would otherwise go into landfills.

A Miracle in Progress

Back Door Brigade

~ by Ann Howard, volunteer

First of all, it is important to understand the role of the men at the back door. Our "boys," as we so fondly refer to them, are vital to the shop's operation. Please understand that the term *boys* is used loosely, as most of them are 50 plus years old, and many are retired. However, they do the work of 20-year-olds. We count these volunteers as some of our most valuable assets and, indeed, our blessings.

Not only do they receive donations at the back door, but they also cart them in for pricing, then haul the heavier items to the sales floor and to customers' vehicles. These men, like mailmen, work all day in heat, rain, sleet, and snow.

Though unpaid, back door volunteers, Jerry Ward (left) and Dean Recktenwall work in all kinds of weather.

A Miracle in Progress

With all of their hard work in varying weather conditions, they must also be our goodwill ambassadors. When people bring us their donations, but do not come inside to browse or shop, these men are their only contact with the shop. To many, they are the "Face" of Resale.

This story comes from one of these unsung heroes, a well-educated professional man and dedicated volunteer. One blustery, cold day he was wearing a heavy, well-worn jacket and an old torn pair of jeans, which were probably soiled from carrying in bags which had sat outside.

After he unloaded a woman's donations, she said, "Well, I truly thank you, sir." Giving him a compassionate look, she continued, "Now, here. You take this." She put a ten dollar bill in his hand.

"Well, thank you, ma'am," he said, "but could you please give the money to one of the cashiers at the front? They handle all the money."

"Oh, no. . . no," she said, "you take it. You know, we always try to help the homeless."

I must look worse than I thought, he mused. Struggling to keep his composure, he said, "Uh. . . no, really, you need to give it to the cashier."

Clearly she was not to be sidetracked. "No, I insist. You take it, and, please, please, whatever you do, don't spend it on drugs or alcohol."

"Well, thank you," he said, and walked away grinning to put the cash into the donation jar.

A Miracle in Progress

Sanford

~ *by Ann Howard, volunteer*

One day, on my way to work at Duneland Resale, I turned the corner and pulled up behind a pickup truck spilling over with a conglomeration of "stuff," which swayed and bounced as the truck moved along. "Oh. . . my. . . goodness!" I said, and laughed at the sight.

What a mess it was! It reminded me of a large porcupine, with broom and mop handles, rakes, sweeper handles, and poles haphazardly sticking out in all directions. So I proceeded cautiously, hoping that none of it would fall out into my path. *That truck must be on its way to the dump,* I thought.

The farther I drove, the more I realized that the truck and I were headed in the same direction. *Oh, I hope that guy isn't going to the shop. It's been such a busy week, and it would take forever to unload all of it,* I thought. The truck turned left. Then I turned left. Block by block, we drove in tandem until I had the sinking feeling that we had to be going to the same place. Sure enough, the truck turned right, and then I turned, right behind it, into the parking lot of Duneland Resale.

I had been so preoccupied watching that unwieldy load in the back of the truck that I had not even bothered to look at the driver. When he

A Miracle in Progress

climbed out of the truck, I gasped, realizing that it was none other than our esteemed Director, Dan Johnston. In the instant that we saw each other, we both laughed out loud, and we could not stop. We laughed until we doubled over and wiped the tears from our eyes.

Finally regaining composure, Dan said, "Just call me Sanford!" And then we "lost it" again. We refer to the incident often, and we have the picture document it.

As it turned out, it was the arrangement of the load and not the load itself that was a mess. It contained some good, saleable items. If there's a moral here, it is that one can't judge a book by its cover. If there's no moral at all, that's just fine, too. We had a great laugh that day, and who doesn't need a great laugh now and then?

"Sanford's" truck and trailer.

A Miracle in Progress

Snippets

*~ as told by volunteers
 to Ann Howard*

Say What?

A woman was trying on clothing at Resale. Dress in hand, she asked, "Do you have this dress in a size 5?"

Another customer asked a volunteer, "Do you sell stamps?"

And then there was the customer who said, "Now, where's the Lane furniture section in this store?"

Anne Inherst related this story. Duneland Resale has over 95 volunteers doing their various tasks to make the shop run. Some work on the sales floor, and many work behind the scenes in the back room. In this area are sorters, pricers and taggers.

A customer remarked that she was amazed at the amount of merchandise available and the work that must be involved. Holding up a price tag, she said, "Now, tell me, just how many hookers do you people have working back there?"

A Miracle in Progress

Guess Again

After Ed Lewandowski helped an older couple unload their donations from their trunk, he asked the standard question: "Would you like a tax receipt?"

"Oh, no, it's not necessary, not at all," the man replied.

Scowling, the woman snapped at her husband, "Just what do you mean?" Then, to Ed, she said, "Oh, yes indeed – it IS necessary. You bet we'll take a receipt!"

"Okay, okay," said the man, "we'll take it." Then he shook his head, looked at Ed and said, "You know, we got married 67 years ago, and she hasn't changed one bit!"

Ed, stifling a grin, retreated quickly to get the controversial receipt.

Who's on First?

A Resale customer asked Chuck Swickard to look at a lamp. She pointed to the label indicating the date the item was checked and the guarantee that it worked, and she asked, "Now, what does this mean?"

He said, "Well, that means it works."
"Does that mean it's okay?" she asked.
"Yes, it works. It's okay," he said.
"You say it's okay?" she asked.

A Miracle in Progress

"Yes, it's okay," he said.
"Then it works?"
"It works."
"Okay, then," she said. She picked up the lamp and walked away.
Chuck scratched his head. "O-o-okay, then," he said and walked into the back room.

A Bargain, More or Less

We all know that Duneland Resale usually offers the best buys in town. Bonnie Flatz, delighted to find numerous packages of Christmas boxes for only 50 cents each, splurged and bought 18 packages of them.

Much to her surprise, she discovered later that a local store had the same packaged boxes on sale for 25 cents each. So much for her bargain-hunting skills!

She was tempted, but did not return her purchase to Resale. "If there's a moral to this story," she said, "it is this: The $9.00 I spent was used to do something good for a person in need. So the packages were a bargain, after all!"

Uh-Oh!

A woman drove up to the Resale Donations door, and then got out of her car to help Ed Lewandowski unload her many items from the

A Miracle in Progress

trunk. After they had finished, he asked if she would like a receipt, and she answered that, *yes*, she would. He went to get one.

When he returned with the receipt, he was surprised to see her sitting in the passenger seat. He must have looked puzzled as he walked around the car to hand it to her, but she apparently did not notice. She simply smiled and thanked him.

He stood there for a few moments, wondering if he should say something, when suddenly, she said, "Oh! Wait! I was the driver, wasn't I?" Looking nonplussed, she threw open the door, rushed around to the driver's side, got in and drove away. Ed was still laughing as he told the story.

Walk the Talk

Every week Bonnie Flatz volunteers at Resale. She and her sister Debbie Wood, whom I have nicknamed the Whiz Sisters because of their speed and efficiency at tagging and hanging clothing, can quickly reduce the mountains of piled up garments to mere foothills.

Although she rarely takes a break, Bonnie still manages to go home with a bag or two of treasures she has bought. Each time, her husband Jerry chides her about "dragging home more stuff that you most likely don't need."

A Miracle in Progress

Then Jerry became a volunteer at the shop. He carries items in and out, taking the heavier ones to the sales floor and carrying bulkier purchases out the back door. Consequently, he goes almost everywhere in the shop and has the opportunity to look around.

One day an amazing thing happened. Jerry proudly went home with a treasure he had found at Resale, something he simply had to have.

Bonnie was overjoyed when she told this story. She said, "He doesn't dare bug me anymore about my purchases. Now he is ONE OF US!

A Miracle in Progress

SIX
Donations

Something Good

~ as told to Ann Howard, volunteer

It was over. After his brave struggle with declining health, he had died. As unreal as it seemed, he was gone, and the tumult of emotions that had overwhelmed her for so long had settled into a quiet grief. She had existed in this vacuum long enough.

She knew that it was time to tackle those chores one must face after such a loss, and she decided to begin with his clothes. As she sorted through his handsome wardrobe, she admired each piece and savored the memories it evoked. *Such a bittersweet task*, she mused, but she kept on, until the last piece had been folded and put into its proper pile.

Some good must come out of all of this, she thought. *Of course, I'll donate them to Duneland Resale. Someone will purchase them and make good use of them, and the money raised from them will be used for charity.*

A Miracle in Progress

Easier said than done, she admitted, as she drove carload after carload of clothing to the shop. After the last load was delivered, she was tired, but relieved. She had done the right thing.

Sometime later, as she sat in church, a man walked past her down the aisle. He was nicely dressed and wore a stunning and distinctive shirt which she instantly recognized. It was one of her husband's, one that she had donated to Resale. Suddenly, she felt a surge of joy and then satisfaction. Out of tragedy and sadness had come something truly good.

A Miracle in Progress

Donations de Jour

~ *as told by volunteers
to Ann Howard, volunteer*

Donations are, of course, our lifeblood, and we are constantly grateful for the generosity of the Duneland community. We receive many donations that are meaningful to our donors.

One donation which touched our hearts was a frosty light blue mid-nineties Buick Le Sabre given to us by two sisters, Alexandra Newman and Paula McHugh. The car had belonged to their mother, Pauline Czarnecki.

Pauline, an enthusiastic supporter of Resale and an ardent shopper, had recently passed away. Having an eye for quality, she had often found real treasures at Resale, her favorite shopping place. Because both sisters are also strong supporters of our mission, they felt moved to donate the car to Duneland Resale.

As a result of their generosity, a fortunate person has now purchased a serviceable car for a reasonable price, and the proceeds from the sale of the car have been used to help those in need.

The Resale mission is also blessed by the memorial monetary donations that we receive in honor of those who have passed away. Each donation – monetary or goods – given to Resale can be thought of as a gift that keeps on giving.

A Miracle in Progress

Agencies and causes receiving help from Duneland Resale, because of these generous donations, are listed in the sections, "Where Does the Money Go?" and "Donations, Duneland Resale Outreach Mission."

Our bequests come in a variety of shapes, sizes, and colors – clothes, furniture, dishes, knickknacks – items which one would expect. However, in the back room it is not unusual to hear, "Oh, my goodness! Would you come and look at this!"

Here are a few of the unique "treasures" that have come to us: a moldy sandwich and to go with it, a bag of potato chips; used tea bags; a provocative lacy, red undergarment, Fredrick's of Hollywood variety, with the sheer red stockings still attached; jeans, legs only, cut off from the pants; high-heeled sneakers; a dog; two lovebirds; a dead mouse; a lamp, which is a statue of a nude figure, waist up; soiled gym clothes; smelly socks; more mouse droppings than one can imagine; vintage mouse traps; dog and cat hair, which, if combined, would be enough to stuff a chair; a used toothbrush; Viagra; several teeth – some good, some with cavities; a gold tooth; a frog, overlooked by us, but discovered by a customer who opened a small box and shrieked as it jumped out and hopped away.

Frank Sessa, our shoe guru, found a rare donation – the perfect pair of shoes for the person

A *Miracle in Progress*

who has two left feet! Rest assured that shoppers will never find most of these items on the sales floor, but discovering them can certainly break the monotony of a humdrum work day!

Sometimes donations are given to us by accident. This donation was likely one of those, and it made us smile. Its innocence transports us back to our childhood days. Who could forget the anticipation of the Tooth Fairy's arrival? This optimistic note was in the same yellowing envelope as several of Billy's teeth:

Dear Fairy Godmother,
I am sorry but I lost one tooth playing baseball and it fell on the ground. I couldn't find it. I went to skating and broke my moller on a totsie roll. It fell out on Tuesday. I put it on my dresser I was cleaning my room for club for my mother and it fell and got mixed up with some other things. So if you want to you can leave me money.
Billy

In another case, Diane Silvonek, a recent mother-of-the-bride who was shopping at the shop discovered a ring bearer's pillow which she was certain had been her daughter's. She continued her shopping and, for the moment, forgot about the pillow. Several days later when she returned, again she saw the pillow. Then a troubling thought

A Miracle in Progress

struck her. She grabbed her cell phone and called her daughter.

"Ronee, it's Mom. Did you donate your ring bearer's pillow to Duneland Resale?"

"Well, I don't know... Did I?" Ronee said.

"You must have. I was just there, looking at it, and I know it's yours. Didn't you promise it to your cousin Lena for her wedding?"

"Oh... Mom, you're right! I did!"

"Don't panic. It's only $10.00. I'll buy it back." Immediately Diane picked up the pillow and found Joy. She told Joy the story and said that she would gladly buy back the pillow.

"Of course you won't buy it," said Joy. "Please take it. It's yours. Thank goodness it was still here!"

Undoubtedly there was a mutual sigh of relief from both women.

One morning a frantic woman called Dan. She had just discovered that her well-meaning children, who had cleaned out a closet and accumulated a sizeable donation for Resale, had inadvertently included a small chest containing their father's ashes.

Dan was not optimistic about finding the box. The shop had been closed during Christmas break, and snow and ice now covered the bags and boxes of donations that had been left outside. Unfortunately, many ruined items had to be thrown away. After digging through piles of soggy, slushy

A Miracle in Progress

items, Dan finally found the chest. He called the woman, who rushed right over.

"Oh, thank you so much, Dan," she said, and then she paused. "Was my husband in the box?"

"Well, all I did was find the box you described, and I never thought to look inside it," Dan said. "I guess that would be up to you."

She quickly lifted the lid and peered inside. Beaming, she said, "He's in there!"

Sometimes our donors surprise us even more than our donations. One most unusual donor we call our celebrity donor. Imagine our delight when a very attractive and personable black and white Shih Tzu named Ollie, accompanied by his owner Vicky Voller, pranced through the door with his donation of clothing.

Vicky Voller and Ollie receive a donation for the Humane Society from Resale volunteer Nancy Ruffing.

A Miracle in Progress

Ollie was rescued and brought to Indiana from the Katrina area by the Humane Society of Northwest Indiana. He was adopted when he was five months old. Vicky thinks that Ollie might be French because he barks with an accent.

Though he is a special needs dog, with a crossed eye and a malformed paw, he has never let his disabilities handicap him. Furthermore, he has a gift – the ability to write. Since January, 2007, he has been writing a weekly column for the *Post-Tribune*, a Duneland area newspaper, and many dogs and cats write to him in hopes that he can solve their problems.

Tee Shirts de Jour

~ *Collected by volunteers*

Many of our donated tee shirts are printed with memorable sayings. Here are some of our favorites:

Everyone is entitled to my opinion.

Those Who Think They Know Everything Annoy Those of Us Who Do!

Sarcasm Is Just One of the Services I Offer!

A Miracle in Progress

Dumpster Diving Team

In Dog Years I'm Dead!

Constant Supervision Required

Heavily Medicated for Your Safety

It's All About Me!

I'm Not Saying You're Stupid, but I'm Glad You Can't Read My Mind!

Keep on Grumpin'
Please Don't Let This Woman Spend Any More Money . . . Her Spouse

Shut Up and Shop!

I Have Major Issues! You've Been Warned!

I Live in My Own Little World, but It's Okay. They Know Me Here.

Contents under Pressure!

I'm Open to Suggestions, as Long as They're Mine
.
Home and Work Are Two Words That Should Never Be Together!

A Miracle in Progress

This Is Where I Nod and Act Like I'm Listening.

Jolly Fat Man with White Beard and Red Suit Seeks Summer Employment!

The Top Ten Reasons Why I Procrastinate: 1... 1...1...

5 Out of 4 People Have Trouble with Fractions.

I'm Immature, Unorganized, Lazy and Loud, but I'm Fun!

Why Don't I Just Drop What I'm Doing and Attend to Your Problems! (a favorite)

A stick figure of a bride and groom were on the front of the shirt, which read: Game Over!

We Do It My Way, or... We Do It My Way!

Will Trade Sister for Video Game

Dear Santa: Let Me Explain...

I Have a Million Excuses. Which One Do You Want to Hear?

A Miracle in Progress

I Can Only Please One Person per Day. This Is Not Your Day!

Make Your Soul Shine!

God Is Like Coke—He's the Real Thing!

SEVEN
Special People
Special Friends

We are blessed with many special people around us – Resale volunteers and special friends within the Duneland community, and we consider them miracles, gifts from God. To tell about them all would fill volumes, and so we include only a few stories.

Many Hats and Herding Cats

~ by Ann Howard, volunteer

Joy Johnston wears many hats, both literally and figuratively, but the one she wears the most is that of Cat Herder.

Nancy Ruffing said, "On our volunteer outing to Chicago, after various stops, people were late boarding the bus. That day, Joy was constantly 'herding cats,' just as she does at the shop. It certainly wasn't a day off for her."

Joy is quick to point out that she does not consider our valuable volunteers as cats, but certainly the coordination of all of the operations and the managing of people doing their specific

A Miracle in Progress

tasks could definitely be considered *herding*. In regard to the volunteers, her job is more like *shepherding*, as she safeguards her flock and also guides them in the right directions, always considerate of their dignity and worth.

The reason that the shop hums along smoothly is Joy's admirable ability to multi-task. As I followed her one busy day, while sorting clothing and facilitating operations in the back room, she was called to the front counter by a frustrated volunteer cashier when the credit card machine refused to work. To add to the confusion, several customers needed furniture carry-outs, but all of the back door volunteers were busy unloading carloads of donations.

Of course, Dan would have gladly helped her, but he was busy pacifying a demanding customer while momentarily ignoring his cell phone, which melodically rang constantly. The cats were certainly yowling that day!

Next, a department chairman asked Joy to help locate some of her items that had been moved from the place she had put them. Just as another volunteer asked for an address to send a sympathy card, Joy was paged to speak to someone inquiring about writing a check to the food pantry. Then she was again flagged down by the cashier to assist with a paper jam. Furthermore, the cashier added that the register tape was running out and there was none to be found behind the counter.

A Miracle in Progress

Joy waved and bantered with smiling customers as she wound her way toward the back room to begin her search for the department chairman's misplaced items. Glancing around, she sighed as she noticed that the dressing rooms were loaded with discarded clothing, toys were strewn everywhere, a pink wad of gum was stuck in the carpeting and the shoes were in complete disarray. The shop, which was in fine shape an hour ago, was now a mess! Just a typical day for herding cats!

When Joy is not herding, she is sorting donations and attending to a variety of other tasks. Even then she is energizing the volunteers and keeping up the morale in the back room, where the work load can be overwhelming.

Although there is ordinarily a relaxed and friendly atmosphere in the back room, at our busiest periods tensions can run high. Just in time, Joy will make her grand entrance, parading through the room with one of her array of eye-catching wigs, hats or unusual attire. Oh, what a sensation she would be in the theater world!

She has many types of hats – mostly large, colorful, and always conversation-stopping – and it is painfully obvious that she is extremely fond of feathers. Sometimes she will fling open the double doors and share her finery with the shoppers. As she saunters through the shop modeling one of her

A Miracle in Progress

favorites, she leaves in her wake a trail of wayward feathers floating aimlessly about.

Joy Johnston and Chance Leady parade through Resale in their crazy, cheesy hats.

Joy's impromptu singing, often compared to Edith Bunker's or the sound of fingernails scraping on a blackboard, can startle the unsuspecting bystander. Her repertoire includes, but is not limited to Girl Scout and camp songs. Some Veggie Tale favorites are: "God Is Bigger than the Boogie Man" and "Where Is My Hair Brush?" as well as the classic oldies. She will perform at the drop of a hat – preferably, one of hers – for all who dare to listen.

She is, indeed, a Joy to Our World!

A Miracle in Progress

Joy Johnston (second from left) is not alone in her love of wearing hats. Left: Bill Gland, Joy, Debbie Wood, Tammie Fero, Gretchen Loomis, Bonnie Flatz.

A Miracle in Progress

Regarding Sanford...

~ *by Ann Howard, volunteer*

Recalling the "Sanford" incident from the "Good Laugh" chapter still makes us chuckle. In truth, Dan Johnston's role at Duneland Resale is much like Sanford's. He is always at the wheel, the capable "driver," with Mrs. Sanford (Joy) right beside him, sharing the responsibility of operating the store. The "load" he carries is also much like Sanford's in its weight and diversity.

Anyone who talks to Dan knows that most of his conversations are punctuated by the music of his cell phone. In addition to answering questions and helping others, he fixes cash registers and credit card machines, hauls furniture and donations in and out and deals with various crises that arise, such as shortages of change for the cash registers, overflowing toilets in the shop, and fender benders in the parking lot.

Dan is busy outside the shop as well. No job is too small for him to tackle. At times he may be seen mowing the grass in front or tidying up the donations area in the back. Managing our various renovation projects, he frequently purchases, then delivers construction supplies to our buildings, often on his days off. (We wonder if he actually has any days off.)

A Miracle in Progress

Of course, he also participates in various Duneland area improvement projects, such as Rebuilding Together. As Resale's liaison to the Duneland community, he attends many meetings and charitable functions. Often he sheds his work clothes and dons his go-to-meeting clothes to dash off to these gatherings. Luckily, he cleans up well, and quickly!

Dan is in perpetual motion. Obviously, his working hours, often starting as early as 5:00 a.m. and ending well past dinnertime, are much longer than our store hours. To follow him around for even one day is exhausting. Still, he manages to have a ready smile and kind words for those around him. One can easily understand why Dan is one of our Special People.

A Miracle in Progress

Pastor Ed

~ as told by Joy Johnston to Ann Howard

Pastor Ed Mitchell was a powerful force in the lives of many people and an inspiration for all those at Duneland Resale. Serving as the Resale Board's first president, he brought his strong Christian faith as well as his experience as an officer in the Salvation Army to the Board.

Pastor Ed (right) and JoAnn and Bob Ruppenkamp

Pastor Ed stressed that the Resale mission should be all about people and cautioned the Board to avoid "getting wrapped up in all the other stuff." His positive attitude was contagious, fostering self-confidence in those around him. One way or

A Miracle in Progress

another, he would find a way to help people meet their challenges.

His sense of humor uplifted the spirits of so many. People still smile as they relate the story of his naming his dog Ed Gr-r-r. Even when his hope of beating cancer waned, his upbeat attitude prevailed. Pastor Ed "walked the talk," and his influence still is strongly felt by many.

Joy Johnston's eulogy for Pastor Ed follows, along with the poem she shared.

"Pastor Ed's mission in life was helping others. He believed people can better themselves and improve their situations with a little help and encouragement. Caring came naturally to him.

Whether you met him at Sand Creek or Spring Valley Homeless Shelter, he treated all persons with equal respect and dignity.

His place of work was more than Porter United Methodist Church... His sermons could be seen on any given day... perhaps at the gas station... buying a scruffy person a Pepsi, petting their dog, chatting about sports, but eventually addressing their addiction and where to find help.

He delivered Meals on Wheels to lonely seniors, volunteered at Duneland Resale, and his wife Linda often had to buy him another winter coat, hat and gloves, because he had given his away to someone who was cold.

Ed served his God and this community by serving others.

A Miracle in Progress

*I'd Rather See A Sermon**

~ by Edgar A. Guest

I'd rather see a sermon
than hear one any day;
I'd rather one should walk with me
than merely tell the way.
The eye's a better pupil
and more willing than the ear,
Fine counsel is confusing,
but example's always clear;
And the best of all preachers
are the men who live their creeds,
For to see good put in action
is what everybody needs.
I soon can learn to do it
if you'll let me see it done;
I can watch your hands in action,
but your tongue too fast may run.
And the lecture you deliver
may be very wise and true,
But I'd rather get my lessons
by observing what you do;
For I might misunderstand you
and the high advice you give,
But there's no misunderstanding
how you act and how you live.

* Public Domain

A Miracle in Progress

True Success

~ *by Ann Howard, volunteer*

Lorrie Woycik is a good friend of Duneland Resale. Both Special Olympics and Opportunity Enterprises are among the causes to which Resale donates.

Lorrie Woycik, an Earth Angel, devotes her life to helping others. She is the Coordinator for Special Olympics and she sits on the Opportunity Enterprises Board, as well as working with the Relay for Life, The United Way and a variety of other charitable organizations. In addition, she has a ministry for handicapped adults.

With all else that she does, she continues to teach swimming to special needs children in order to help them gain strength and develop other physical skills. Obviously, Lorrie has enough love in her heart to share with many people.

Her own words best express her philosophy for success in life: "So many people equate success with having lots of money, expensive cars and grand houses, and they are so off the mark. Success is your knowing that something you did brought joy to someone's life. That success you keep with you, and all the rest is temporary. For me, success is hearing one of the little ones say, 'I missed you when you were gone, Miss Lorrie,' or,

A Miracle in Progress

'Miss Lorrie, I love you and I'm so glad you're here.' The more you give, the more you receive, and I am truly blessed."

Those who are touched by Lorrie's kindness are also truly blessed.

Lorrie Woycik (white hat) and Andy Petrovich enjoy riding in a community parade.

A Miracle in Progress

The Hungry Are Fed

~ *by Ann Howard, volunteer*

Our friends, Joan and Loren Knibbs, coordinators of Westchester Neighbors Food Pantry, have given over 22 years of service to our community. Many experiencing difficult times have food on their tables and in their cupboards because of these dedicated people and their fellow volunteers.

Earth Angels Joan and Loren Knibbs

Every two weeks nearly 123 families are given groceries, and the numbers are increasing.

A Miracle in Progress

At Christmas in 2009, 199 families were helped. From January through September 2010, 8,086 people have received food from the Food Pantry, which is now housed in the west side of our building at 801 Broadway.

Joan's other charitable mission is the Duneland Medical Equipment Loan Closet, also located in the west side of our building. This organization lends recycled medical equipment to those who need it. Right now Joan has over 400 pieces of equipment in her inventory. What a blessing it is for one to be able to borrow crutches, a walker, a wheel chair or other necessary equipment during times of illness!

The Knibbs are certainly Earth Angels.

A Miracle in Progress

Alyce

~ *by Ann Howard, volunteer*

First, a flash of red, and then – poof! Alyce Bruhn-Scott appears. Usually clad in red from head-to-foot, this free spirit dances through the front door of Resale. She wears a hat – red, of course, or sometimes red, white, and blue, and definitely outlandish – and a broad, contagious smile.

Alyce Bruhn-Scott and Joy Johnston burst into song together at the third Resale shop.

She makes a grand entrance, often bursting forth with a song in her Gravel Gertie voice – "Happy Days Are Here Again" or something equally lively. Frequently she offers us a tidbit of wisdom, such as: "Love many; trust few. Always

A Miracle in Progress

paddle your own canoe." At times she recites an upbeat poem. Certainly, she is never predictable.

How old is Alyce? She does not say, and we do not ask. After all, whether or not to share such private information is a woman's prerogative. Her wizened face and white hair tell us that she is no longer young, at least not in years. However, her heart is another matter. She is the youngest at heart of almost anyone we know.

When she sings, or recites a ditty, or does a jig, she is a girl again. And she takes us with her – back to a more carefree time, when we were young. If only for a few minutes, we are children again; we forget our worries and take ourselves less seriously. What a refreshing change!

Alyce, a retired minister, firmly believes that the proverbial glass is half full, and she radiates that optimism. She is a lover of people and an enthusiastic celebrator of life, and it is no surprise that she is well-known and warmly greeted wherever she goes.

But don't be fooled. Half imp, half sage, she can discuss politics or world affairs as easily as she can entertain and delight us. Most important, Alyce brings us the gift of joy. And sometimes, she even brings us cookies. Shine on, Alyce!

A Miracle in Progress

Miss Martha

~ *by Ann Howard, volunteer*

Martha Reynolds, our friend who has now passed, was ninety-some years old and quite young at heart. A free spirit, she lived in a cottage on the beach and loved friends, nature, music, art and Duneland Resale. She was a frequent customer at the shop and enjoyed visiting with the people there and ducking into the kitchen to sample the ever-present array of goodies.

Joy Johnston and Martha Reynolds chat at Resale.

When the shop had outgrown its third space and we were searching for a larger place, early on Martha decided that we should purchase the former Wiseway grocery store building.

A Miracle in Progress

We agreed that the building would be perfect, but there were several years when acquiring Wiseway seemed to be a pipe dream. Martha, a woman of faith, never gave up and prayed constantly for our success.

With a conspiratorial glimmer in her eye and a raised eyebrow, she would lean in closely and whisper, "Well? Did you get the Wiseway yet?"

"No, not yet," we would answer.

"Well, don't worry. You will, dear. You will!" she would say.

Martha was a staunch believer in the power of God to work miracles and she had great faith in God's timing. Surely Martha is smiling down at us, knowing that she was exactly right about God's plan for Duneland Resale.

A Miracle in Progress

Charlie's Gift

~ by Ann Howard, volunteer

Our friend Charlie is no longer with us. He was, as we all are, on loan from God. Charlie was an Autistic Savant, and he constantly amazed us all. The moment he entered the Resale shop, he looked for Joy, who would give him a Coke. Oh, how he loved both Joy and those Cokes!

Charlie was extremely outgoing and always eager to demonstrate his remarkable talent. There was a regular routine. Joy or his caregiver would say to a volunteer or customer, "Charlie would like to show you what he can do, if it's okay with you. You'll be so impressed."

Pleased, he would ask, "Can you tell me what day, month and year were you born?"

The person would answer, "I was born on June 25, 1950, but why do you . . ."

Before the question was finished, he would say, "Your next birthday will be on a Wednesday." And he was always correct. Of course, customers were surprised and delighted, and he was very happy with his remarkable feat – rightly so.

Charlie is gone, but we will always remember his enthusiasm and his unique gift.

A Miracle in Progress

Walking Softly

~ *as told by Dan Johnston, volunteer,*
  to Ann Howard, volunteer

We have wonderful memories of Shirley Keller, our dedicated volunteer who has passed away. Shirley was so passionately devoted to the Resale mission that, in the early days, she anonymously paid the water bills.

We can still picture Shirley looking sweet and motherly in her cozy granny nightgown at our Midnight Madness sale. But as we all know, looks can be deceiving.

Shirley Keller (left), Chuck Swickard, and Madeline Rhoda-Brush have fun at the Midnight Madness sale.

Back when the shop was located on Calumet Avenue, each day Shirley insisted on walking the

A Miracle in Progress

short distance to the bank to deposit the daily proceeds. Fearing for her safety, Joy cautioned her that she was an easy target and urged her to ask another volunteer to accompany her. Shirley gave Joy a direct, determined look, which seemed to say, "You do it your way, and I'll do it mine," and she continued her daily deliveries. . . solo.

While checking out customers, Shirley often sat on a stool behind the cash register. From her kind expression and gentle manner, the customer would never suspect that she kept a baseball bat beside her, "just in case. . ." Undoubtedly, Shirley believed that it is wise to "Walk softly and carry a big stick."

EIGHT
Reflections

Teamwork

~ *by Ann Howard, volunteer*

What a spirit of teamwork we have at Duneland Resale! Different people with a variety of backgrounds, personalities, and interests come together with a common purpose and mesh into an effective work force. The back room itself is an example of teamwork at its best. To see the activity on an ordinary day is like being inside of a beehive, with each different worker, attending to his or her individual task while cooperating with the others to ready the items for the sales floor.

Team participation in community events strengthens the bonds among our volunteers. Each year we join with others in Rebuilding Together to build, paint, rake or do any necessary tasks to help people maintain their homes, or to enhance designated community areas. The day can be exhausting, but working side by side with friends, both old and new, and enjoying the conversation and banter among the volunteers make the tasks both fulfilling and enjoyable.

A Miracle in Progress

Don Pratt works on a home for Rebuilding Together.

The annual American Cancer Society's Relay for Life is another exciting event for our team. One year's theme was Hollywood, and Mark Ligda, with the help of several other creative volunteers, devised stunning decorations which included the red carpet, a giant Oscar, gold stars with the names of Cancer survivors, tips for avoiding cancer and other imaginative touches.

Our team of approximately 100 volunteers, customers, and friends walked the track around the clock. Because so many of our lives have been

A Miracle in Progress

touched by cancer, the Relay for Life is a poignant and unforgettable experience for all.

Teamwork is also important in raising money for the Relay for Life. We recently held our first Bark for Life, featuring a dog walk, booths of pet supply vendors, rescue groups, a bake sale for pets and their owners, and more. Pet identification chips were provided at a discount. Nearly 70 dogs and their owners enjoyed the event, which turned out to be a huge success – no woofing!

The Resale team walks in the annual Crop Walk.

Other walks in which we have participated include the C.A.D.C. (Community Action Drug Coalition) Walk and the C.R.O.P. (Communities Responding to Overcome Poverty) Hunger Walk. In 2009 Kim Goldak organized a team of

A Miracle in Progress

volunteers to man a sandwich stand at the local OZ Fest to raise additional funds for the CROP Walk.

Lee Swink heard about the White Castle Olympiad, a hamburger cook-off in the Chicago area. After this competition, the burgers were frozen and distributed to those in need.

Lee approached Dan Johnston and said, "Let's have an Olympiad for our local food pantry."

Dan agreed and Lee obtained permission from the Northwest Indiana White Castle to hold the event. Dan made many calls and organized the event. Volunteer cooks were recruited, and the fun began. The competition, which was held for several years, was very successful. All the burgers were frozen and given to the Westchester Neighbors Food Pantry.

When Joan Knibbs, who is Food Pantry Coordinator, was asked how many burgers were passed out, she said, "Hundreds! Just hundreds!"

Certainly there was no "beef" when the many Duneland families received their burgers!

Our Second Chance Singers join together for six weeks of practice for the annual Duneland Community Advent Festival, which is held each year on the second Friday of December. This event features a dozen or more church choirs who perform for the community.

A Miracle in Progress

Linda Handlon directs the Second Chance Singers at the annual Duneland Community Advent Festival at St. Patrick's Church.

Coordinator Michael Boo said: "This event is Duneland's gift to itself."

Not only does the community enjoy the lovely music, but also the entire goodwill offering benefits the local Food Pantry. Each year Resale has matched this offering.

Our long-time volunteer and brave song leader, Linda, starts with a rag-tag bunch of singers and, in record time, with patience and skill transforms us into an acceptable choir. We like to think that where our quality is lacking, our enthusiasm compensates. We can only hope that others agree.

A Miracle in Progress

Volunteers join residents at The Waters of Duneland for Christmas caroling.

Each year Linda also leads us as we sing Christmas carols and hand out balloons to the residents of a local nursing home. Some join in the singing or walk along with us, and many smile or wipe away a tear as they listen. All of us, no matter how distracted we are by the hurried atmosphere of the holidays, are filled with the Christmas spirit on this occasion. Duneland Resale is an example of teamwork at its best!

A Miracle in Progress

Celebration

~ by Ann Howard, volunteer

"Attention, all shoppers! We have another 100 percent off purchase!" a jovial voice booms out over the microphone. An explosion of cheering, shouting, and clapping fills the room as another customer gets an unbelievable discount, and each shopper hopes that he or she will be the next big winner.

Ivy Tech Night, a Resale event which ushers in the holiday season, is anticipated by volunteers and customers alike. For one night in early December, our volunteer Jack Schoenfelder brings in his energetic and enthusiastic Ivy Tech Marketing and Management students to run the shop.

Jack Schoenfelder and his business management class work the Ivy Tech Night celebration.

A Miracle in Progress

Delighted shoppers munch on yummy Christmas cookies and treats while live music entertains them and laughter echoes throughout the shop.

Before checking out, customers draw slips listing the amount of their discounts, which can be 25, 50, 75, or even the ultimate 100 percent. Santa's hearty "Ho, ho, ho's" add to the fun as he hears the Christmas wishes of all the small, and also the grown-up boys and girls who have been good all year long.

Anna Hall (left) and Rosemarie Bodnar tell Santa Dave they've been good Resale volunteers all year.

The merriment on Ivy Tech Night is contagious, and this grand evening is enjoyed by all who attend.

A Miracle in Progress

All Work and No Play? Not for Us!

~ *by Ann Howard, volunteer*

Obviously Duneland Resale is a very busy place. The work there is never-ending, but do not think for a minute that we volunteers do not have our share of fun, too.

We can always take the time to stop and smell the. . . lasagne, sloppy Joes, or whatever awaits us in the kitchen, our gathering place. Among their other attributes, many of our volunteers and friends are good cooks, and the kitchen table often holds an array of culinary delights, such as doughnuts, brownies, cookies, cakes and more. Coffee, pop, and snacks are always there for us at break or lunchtime.

We celebrate birthdays with singing and cake; often we present those honored with gag gifts. Of course, there are no complaints when Resale treats us to pizza parties!

Dean and Joyce Recktenwall, husband and wife volunteers, once treated us to malted milk shakes, and it's no surprise that there are requests for an encore. Jerry Ward's Reuben sandwiches also made quite a hit with the volunteers.

Resale anniversaries are celebrated with the public, with special sales to commemorate them. Various holidays such as St. Patrick's Day, Halloween and even the Chinese New Year are

A Miracle in Progress

festive occasions, with decorations and sometimes costumes, ranging from simple to elaborate. Halloween in particular brings out an assortment of characters, and we have the photos as evidence. We have Virgo days and other theme days, which rally enthusiastic support. Picture, if you dare, volunteers clad in makeshift togas and leafy headbands – a sight to behold!

Volunteers in costumes spread fun at Halloween. Left: Chris Medley, Sandra Shrader, Dan Keilman, Ray Tamborski, Joy Johnston, John Komenas.

One day, Billy Wayne, who was doing repairs for us, stopped in for lunch. He had brought his guitar and began to sing. That lunch turned into a jovial sing-along; some of the customers heard the music and joined in the fun. We learned that Billy is a local entertainer who sings, plays a

A Miracle in Progress

"mean" guitar, and does over 200 impressions. Hearing his impersonation of Elvis singing "Love Me Tender" would make one swear that Elvis has definitely NOT left the building!

Special events are planned as a thank-you to our volunteers. Ross Blythe, a retired college professor and volunteer, has led several delightful bus trips to Chicago and the environs. Ross has a vast knowledge of Chicago, its geography and history, and as a bonus, he also has a wonderful sense of humor. We are never bored during our trips because Ross not only keeps us informed, but also keeps us laughing.

Several years ago 20 of our volunteers took a cruise to the Caribbean. A great time was had by all, and many are hoping for another volunteer cruise in the future.

Volunteers have enjoyed productions at the Fourth Street Theater in Chesterton. There is talk of a possible future trip to see a play in Chicago.

A festive spring gala with music, dinner, and dancing gave us a chance to relax and socialize with our fellow workers and friends in the community. The price was right, the food was delicious, the band was fantastic, and the company was the best! We at Duneland Resale can never say that it's all work and no play for us!

A Miracle in Progress

Behind the Scenes

~ by Joy Johnston, volunteer

Lasting impressions. . .
- Humbling is feeling a small child hugging my leg, her tiny voice saying, "Thank you for my bed. . . I don't sleep on the floor anymore." (She is one of three children whose mother was dying of cancer, being raised by grandma living only on social security.)
- Seeing three little children without gloves or hats, a senior in a wheel chair with oxygen tank in tow, waiting outdoors in a very long line to receive groceries from the local food pantry and vowing that "one day," if the Resale succeeds, our neighbors could at least be sheltered from the rain and snow.
- Seeing the vision come true years later, through the *hard work* of each and every dedicated Duneland Resale volunteer. The Resale's community center complete with various social services under one roof – especially the food pantry.
- Hearing that a grandson saved his allowance and birthday money to buy a three-wheeled bike from Resale to give to a neighbor suffering from Multiple Sclerosis.

A Miracle in Progress

- Assisting a family to transport their child for medical treatment at Riley hospital by discreetly giving them gas cards for the trip. Just one of the numerous families in crisis whose dignity ws preserved by Duneland Resale's anonymous giving in their time of need.
- Watching retired Resale men set aside their titles of coach, Dr., mill supervisor, school principal, bank president, attorney, etc., to join the Resale cause by fixing toys, electrical items, greeting customers, carrying in donations from donors. . . choosing to help those in need, while still enjoying the golf course.
- Realizing the amazing power within Resale's "We can do it!" women. Some are in their 90's, but all posses unwavering ENTHUSIASM and resiliency. They really *are* changing our world. . . one recycled sweater at a time.
- Glimpsing the ripples of God's love putting faith into action everyday at Duneland Resale.

A Miracle in Progress

NINE
Just the Facts

Did You Know . . .

Some facts as told by volunteer Joy Johnston, and some as found in the Resale volunteer handbook:

Did you know that . . .

Resale often "dresses" contestants for the YMCA's Womanless Beauty Pageant?

Theater groups such as the Fourth Street Players come to Resale to find costumes?

Some lawyers have asked Resale to help "dress" their clients for court?

Westchester Public Library, our local library, comes to Resale to find items for their displays?

Our Outreach Mission has financially assisted hundreds of families in need?

Most families never know from whom the assistance came?

A Miracle in Progress

Over 95 volunteers spend at least 3 hours working at Resale each week?

Our volunteers are from 20 various community churches?

Resale receives no financial support from any church or agency?

Volunteers (via the volunteer meetings) have input as to what projects are sponsored?

Resale volunteers pay for all of their purchases, and they pay the price listed, just as any other customer?

Resale has helped Portage and several other charitable resale shops get started? In addition, Resale passed on its unused $3000 start-up money to Portage.

People have asked: "If Resale is an outreach mission, why do you charge customers? Why not simply give away items to those in need?"
Answer: *If there is no profit, we would not be able to pay medical expenses, rents, utility bills, and emergency needs for those who cannot pay; furthermore, we would be unable to meet the*

A Miracle in Progress

considerable expenses of running and maintaining the resale shop.

People have asked: "What happens in the event someone cannot afford even your low prices?"
Answer: *Those who have been screened by clergy, social workers and other agencies and found to be in dire need are given gift certificates to protect their anonymity and dignity.*

People have asked: "Why are recipients of your donations screened by clergy and others?"
Answer: *To be good stewards of the money that Resale earns from the sale of your donations, entrusted to us, we must be sure that those helped are truly in need.*

The Resale Board gratefully burns the mortgage for the 534 Broadway shop. Seated left: Ann Howard, Mary Louise Reey. Standing left: Joyce Recktenwall, Jack Schoenfelder, Joy Johnston, Dan Johnston, Dan Keilman, Bill Ong. Not pictured: Kim Goldak.

A Miracle in Progress

Recycling Goods to Do Good

*~ by Ann Howard, volunteer,
with information from the Resale handbook*

As Kermit the Frog said, "It ain't easy being green," but easy or not, we keep on trying!

Recycling is at the heart of our Resale mission. To quote from our mission statement: "Quality used clothing and merchandise which is donated to us is *recycled* and sold. Proceeds are used to assist service agencies, missions, and community needs."

Good items which we are unable to use are donated to other service agencies, missions or individuals in need, such as the homeless, or they are recycled in an environmentally friendly way. At our request, the county's Solid Waste Disposal Agency has audited our trash and recommended the best ways for us to recycle it.

At one time we supplied many of our customers with recyclable shopping bags and cards, which were stamped each time the bags were used. After ten stamps, the customers received a discount on their purchases. We continue to look at ways to entirely eliminate the use of plastic bags in our shop.

Joy reminds us that "Every day is Earth Day at Duneland Resale."

A Miracle in Progress

The following is a list of places where our unused items are donated:

Afghans: Mission
Aluminum cans: Duneland Recycling
Baby gear: NW Women's Center
Beauty supplies: Caring Place
Bikes: Boys & Girls Clubs and Michigan City Prison Project
Blankets: animal shelters
Books: Westchester Public Library, missions, Military in Iraq, Food Pantry
Bric-a-brac: Recycling Center, Hammond
Cardboard: Duneland Recycling
Cell phones: Caring Place and S.A.D.D.
Clothing and miscellaneous items: Salvation Army
Diapers: Women's Center & Food Pantry
Glasses: Lions Club
Housewares and Furniture: Spring Valley Shelter
Medical equipment: Duneland Medical Equipment
Loan Closet: Joan Knibbs
Men's Clothing: Men's shelters and Prison Mission
Metal (unusable): recycling
Paper/catalogues:* Newsprint Retriever
Woolen sweaters: P. Wheelock, pet toys and items

*There is a paper recycling container in the Resale parking lot.

A Miracle in Progress

Where Does the Money Go?

~ *by Ann Howard, volunteer*

So many customers have asked where the Duneland Resale money and in-kind donations go. There is no short answer to the question. Although we have displayed a list of our charitable donations, it is impossible to keep it up to date. This section is a general overview of the variety of donations made since our mission began.

Bill Ong, treasurer, is a good steward of Duneland Resale's finances.

Our proceeds help a multitude of good causes – a new kidney for a six-year-old local girl; medical assistance for people with terminal

A Miracle in Progress

diseases or severe injuries; clothing and household goods for fire victims; a new van to transport American Legion Veterans to the Veterans' Hospital; bracelets equipped with tracking devices to help the Sheriff's Department find Alzheimer patients or otherwise mentally challenged people; prescription medicines for health care facilities; clothing for prison and other ministries, and for local and foreign missions; and monies for utility, rent and other bills for those in need as requested by clergy, Township Trustees and social workers.

Resale often holds fund-raisers for those needing assistance to meet the high costs of medical bills. One example was a benefit for Ellen Clendenin, a friend of many in the community, who was fighting cancer.

A nurse at the Porter Hospital Detox Unit calls upon us regularly for funds for those with mental problems or chemical dependency who are in need of a half-way house. We regularly donate to area shelters and soup kitchens and give out gift certificates as needed. Over $6,000 in certificates are passed out at holiday time to the local Food Pantry and to churches requesting them.

Our Director and several other volunteers have made trips to provide books and gift certificates for building supplies to help with Katrina damage. We have sent funds to organizations aiding hurricane victims in Haiti.

A yearly donation to the Chesterton Art

A Miracle in Progress

Center helps to provide free art classes to over 300 developing artists each year, including 75 to 85 senior citizens. The Center's youth programs include Girl and Boy Scout projects and children's art classes, such as drawing, fabric art, stained glass, photography, and matting and framing.

Here is an example of how this donation has brought unexpected benefits. A friend of one of our volunteers lost her husband and came into very difficult times, emotionally and financially. She took a free art class at the center and over time developed her talent to a remarkable extent. Now her artwork is displayed throughout our area.

For a more detailed list of Resale's donations, please refer to the following chapter.

A Miracle in Progress

Duneland Resale Outreach Mission

This list is as complete as possible as of publication.

Alcoholics Anonymous
Alice's House
ALS Disease Research
Alzheimer Association
American Cancer Society (Relay for Life)
American Diabetes Association
American Foundation for Suicide Prevention
American Heart Association
American Legion
American Red Cross
Asthma Camp
Autism Research
Avon Walk for Breast Cancer

Loretta Lach (left) accepts a donation for the Share Foundation from Lu Paulson, Resale volunteer.

A Miracle in Progress

Benefits for those injured &/or ill
Brain Cancer Research
Boys & Girls Club, Porter County
Boy Scouts of America
Bradley Center
Campus Life
Candle Lighters (Children with Cancer)
Canine Companions
Caring Place
Career Job Fair
Chesterton Adult Learning Center
Chesterton Art Center
Chesterton Fire Department
Chesterton Hometown Improvement Project
Chesterton Park Department
Chesterton Police Department
Chesterton Street Department
Chesterton Tree Committee
Christian Community Action
Christian Food Pantry, Valparaiso, IN
Christian Haven
Christmas for Kids
Church Camp Scholarships
Cleft Connection
Community Action Drug Coalition
Community Prayer Breakfast
Crimestoppers
Crohn's Disease
CROP Walk
Deaf Services of NW Indiana
Diabetes Research
Disabled American Veterans
Discoveries Unlimited
Doctors Without Borders, Haiti relief
Down Syndrome Association of NWI

A Miracle in Progress

Duneland Education Foundation
Duneland Historical Society
Duneland Medical Supply
Duneland Resale Adult Continuing Education Scholarship
Duneland Resale College Scholarships
Duneland Family YMCA
Dunes Fellowship House
Early Intervention
Exceptional Equestrians Unlimited
Faith Communities Men's Overnight Shelter
Family & Youth Services Bureau of Porter County
Family Focus Counseling
Family House
Fellowship House, Michigan City
Fire Victims
First Contact, partnership
Fried's Cat Shelter
Frontline Foundations
Gabriel's Horn
Girl Scouts of America
Goodwill Industries
Greenwich House
Habitat for Humanity, Michigan City, IN
Habitat for Humanity, Valparaiso, IN
Healthline
Heifer Project International
Hilltop House
Hines Veterans Hospital
Hoosier Burn Camp
Hospice of Porter County
Housing Opportunities
Humane Societies
Huntington's Disease Research
Hurricane Disaster Relief, Katrina

A Miracle in Progress

Independent Cat Society
Jacob's Table Soup Kitchen
Juvenile Diabetes Research Foundation
Kids Alive, Haiti Relief
LaPorte County Home
Leader Dogs
Learning Center, National Park
Leukemia
Lions Club White Cane Drive
Loving House Project
Lupus Foundation of America, Research
Lymphoma Association Research
Martin Luther King Youth
Meals on Wheels, Chesterton, Michigan City
Men's Overnight Shelter
Michigan City Homeless Shelter
Michigan City Soup Kitchen
Moraine House
Morningstar Camp, Allergy Dog
Moraine Ridge Wildlife Rehabilitation
Multiple Sclerosis
Muscular Dystrophy Research
National Breast Cancer Foundation
National Hotline for Runaway Children
New Creation Men's Center
Open Door Health Care
Opportunity Enterprises
Pancreatic Cancer Research
Parents as Teachers
PATH
Pathways
Portage Township Food Pantry
Portage Health Care Center
Porter County Cancer Society

A Miracle in Progress

Porter County Council on Aging & Community Services
Porter County Counseling
Porter County Family Nutrition Program
Porter County Mental Health Association
Porter County, Prevent Child Abuse
Porter County Sheriff Department
Porter Fire Department
Rebuilding Together, Duneland
Renewed Horizons (disabled adult day care)
Riley Children's Hospital
Royal Family Kids' Camp
St. Agnes Adult Day Care
St. Jude's Hospital
Salvation Army Food Pantry
Salvation Army, Porter County
Samaritan Counseling
Samaritan's Purse
Share Foundation
Shop with a Cop
Skate Street
Special Equestrians of Porter County
Special Olympics
Spring Valley Homeless Center
St. Jude's Children's Hospital
Stepping Stones Women's Shelter
Supporters of the Military
Table of Plenty Soup Kitchen
Tourette Syndrome Association
Tsunami Relief
Visiting Nurses Association
Westchester Head Start, XXI Geminus
Westchester History Museum
Westchester Public Library
Westchester Neighbors Food Pantry

A Miracle in Progress

Women's Center of Northwest Indiana
Women's Recovery House
Xtreme Sport Club
Youth for Christ
Youth Service Bureau

Resale volunteers Kim Goldak (left), Mary Louise Reey, and Bill Ong ring the Salvation Army Christmas bells.

A Miracle in Progress

Volunteer Service

The names of our deceased volunteers, followed by an asterisk, are included in this list, instead of being listed separately, because they remain in our hearts as a part of the Duneland Resale family.

Pat and Anne Inherst (left) and their sister-in-law Jeanene Inherst at the tree planting in memory of Jeanene's husband and Pat's brother, Bob Inherst.

In compiling this list, we realized that we have only touched the "tip of the iceberg." We have tried to include all those who have supported the mission by their help. We apologize in advance if we have inadvertently overlooked any of your names. We are grateful to you all!

Ailes, Aleta
Amsutz, Lee
Amstutz, Pat
Arnold, Sue
Babcock, Gregory
Banghart, Lorrayne*
Barrett, Louise
Bates, Diana
Bayer, Marie

Bekavac, Nada*
Bennett, Gary
Benninghoff, Linda
Berndt, Lois
Beverly, Jan
Beverly, Vicky
Bishop, Phyllis
Blakely, Joy
Bloom, B.*

A Miracle in Progress

Bloomquist, Amy
Blythe, Phyllis
Blythe, Ross
Bodnar, Rosemarie
Bolesch, Barbara
Bowen, Deborah
Brickner, Evelyn
Brown, Donna
Brush, Madeline Rhoda
Brush, Roy "Shirley"
Beuchley, Paula
Burns, Lynne
Burnside, Karen
Bushore, Carol
Canright, Rosemary
Carlisle, Pat
Cassler, Kim
Chanupa, Dave
Clark, Julia
Clements, Tom
Collins, Evanna
Collins, LeRoy
Collins, Lynn*
Conrad, Matt
Conrad, Pat
Corell, Diann
Dalton, Peggy
Daulbert, Richard
Davis, Emily
Deligatti, Jane
Dickinson, Joan*
Dickinson, Ramona
Diffenbach, Theresa
Dimitroff, Ruth
Doane, Mary

Dolk, Grace
Draves, Kerri
Draves, Rose*
Dunbar, Becky
Dunbar, Bob
Dunn, Bee*
Dunn, Sue
Dybas, Annette
Edds, Sue
Eggers, Al
Evans, David
Evans, John
Evanseck, Sandy
Fero, Brandon
Fero, Josh
Fero, Kerry
Fero, Tammie
Fitzsimmons, Sharon
Flatz, Bonnie
Flatz, Jerry
Fletcher, Stephen
Foster, Irma
Fowler, Lynda
Fulton, Virginia
Galka, Barbara
Gardner, Sheila
Gartner, Ray
Gaston, Al
Gaston, Marcia
Gland, Bill
Goldak, Frank
Goldak, Kim
Goldak, Zach
Gotch, Mike
Gotlind, Phyllis

A Miracle in Progress

Graham, Becky
Gray, Bob*
Gray, Linda
Groves, Diane
Gustafson, Ed
Hall, Anna
Hancock, Billy Wayne
Handlon, Linda
Handlon, Steve
Harris, Michael
Harrison, Molly
Hefner, Mary
Heider, Bob*
Heistand, Ann
Henderson, Helen
Higgins, Chris
Hill, Evelyn
Hillyer, Dave
Hinken, Deborah
Hokanson, Noreen
Holman, Craig
Hopper, Bonnie*
Hopper, Jack
Howard, Ann
Howe, Melissa
Hudspeth, Jayne
Hultman, Maggie
Inherst, Anne
Inherst, Pat
Jackson, Pat
Janosky, Beverly
Jasen, Joan
Jeselnick, Mary Kay
Johnson, Kay
Johnson, Warren

Johnston, Dan
Johnston, Evia
Johnston, Joy
Jones, Carolyn
Jones, Kevin
Jordan, Elizabeth
Kado, Carol
Kalbe, Christi
Kamaski, Mary
Keane, Mary
Keever, Sandra
Keilman, Dan
Keller, Ken
Keller, Shirley*
Kelly, Tom
Kerr, Nancy
Kiegiela, Mary Ann
Kinser, Glenda
Kinser, Marvin
Knibbs, Joan
Knibbs, Loren
Kolstad-Blanchard, Jackie
Komenas, Evelyn
Komenas, John
Kremke, Bob
Kremke, Mary Beth*
Kremke, Jason
Kronland, Deanna
Kuziela Mary Ann
Leady, Adam
Leady, Chance
Leady, Dana
Leady, Ryan
Leu, Yiu-Mei

A Miracle in Progress

Lewandowski, Ed
Lewis, Dwight
Ligda, David
Ligda, Mark
Lindquist, Eleanor*
Lines, Alberta
Loomis, Gretchen
Lukach, Paul
Lukmann, Charles
Mamula, Marianne
Martin, Dennis
Martin, Nancy
Mastile, Lora
Matthys, Rita
Maxwell, Ruth
McCarthy, Brian
McDonald, Pat
McMeans, Julia
McMeans, Lora
McMeans, Marty
Medley, Christine
Melchiori, John
Melchiori, Sharon
Meyer, Fran*
Micciche, Karen
Miller, Barb
Miller, Theatus
Milosevich, Pat
Mitchell, Ed*
Montgomery, Monty
Moore, Sandy
Morris, Kate
Morris, Roger
Murchek, Connie
Murcheck, Jack

Neel, Roberta
Nelson, Terry*
Novak, Rita
Oberle, Tim
Olson, Roy
Olson, Zella
Ong, Bill
Ong, Nona
Pals, Mary Ann
Pals, Randy
Parker, Debbie
Passarelli, Jeri
Paulson, Lucille
Peterson, Kristy
Petrovich, Andy
Phegley, Carole
Post, Sarah
Pratt, Don
Price, Carol
Ream, Laurie
Rearick, Pam
Recktenwall, Dean
Recktenwall, Joyce
Reey, Mary Louise
Rhoda-Brush, Madeline
Ricca, Harold*
Ricca, Kathleen
Roberts, Lou
Roberts, Tom
Robertson, Emilie,
Rodriquez, Alex
Ross, Jim
Ross, Judy
Rubinate, Delores
Rudzinski, Jennette

A Miracle in Progress

Ruffing, Nancy
Ruhmann, Bruce
Ruppenkamp, Bob
Ruppenkamp, Jo Ann*
Ryan, Sue
Samuelson, Millie
Scharp, Liz
Schilla, Ruth
Schiller, Susan
Schmitt, Jim
Schmitt, Pat
Schoenfelder, Jack
Seiwert, Leanne
Sessa, Frank
Shrader, Sandra
Sievert, Bill
Sievert, Ruby
Simms, Keith
Singer, Ann
Sipe, Nancy
Sitar, Joan
Sjaaheim, Vanessa
Smith, Emilie
Souza, Sheryl
Sprague, Kalen
Sprague, Trish
Steciuch, Florian
Steciuch, Sadie
Sterken, Carol
Strickland, Pam
Sutkowski, Cookie
Swickard, Chuck
Swickard, Lillian
Tarquinee, Terri
Taylor, Bob

Thomas, Mavis
Thorstad, Eric
Thorstad, Laura
Tilden, Marissa
Tilden, Tricia
Tilden, Sam
Trimble, Maurice*
Ulrich, Margo
Ulrich, Paul
Valdivia, Jerry
Valdivia, Ron
Vanderworth, Penny
Wadman, Norman
Wagner, Joe
Wainovich, Joni
Ward, Betty
Ward, Jerry
Warieka, Anne
Weitzel, Deloris
Wells, Dawn Anne
Westergren, Marlene
Whalls, Jim
Whalls, JoAnn
Wheelock, Pam
White, Bill
Whitlow, Barb
Whitlow, Skip
Wiseman Pitts, April
Wood, Debbie
Woods, Ann
Woods, Bob
Woulfe, Joan
Wright, Pat
Zenci, Dorothy
Zink, Alice

A Miracle in Progress

Zella Olson (left) and Joan Sitar, volunteers

By NO means...

THE END

...the journey continues...

All proceeds from the sale of this book benefit Duneland Resale